Around the Edge of the Olympics on a Mountain Bike

A guidebook with 24 rides circling Olympic National Park

by Dave Rowan

"Human beings destroy their ecology at the same time they destroy one another. From that perspective, healing our society goes hand in hand with healing our personal, elemental, connection with the phenomenal world."

—Chögyam Trungpa

ISBN 13: 978-0-9817165-0-3
ISBN 10: 0-9817165-0-4

Library of Congress Control Number: 2008903506

Cover Photo: The view south from Trap Pass.

Dedication

To my father, who told me the first stories I heard about the Olympics.

Acknowledgments

I want to thank the following people for helping me with this project: best friends Gordy Yancey and Tom Kennedy, artists Laurie Geissinger and Jeanne Keckler, editor Jim Whiting, book designer Kathy Campbell at Gorham Printing, U.S. Forest Service employees Pete Erben, Molly Erickson, and Steve McNealy, Charlie Cortelyou of the DNR, Linda Schwartz formerly of the Bicycle Alliance, and most especially counselor and coach Jane Holmes. I also want to voice my appreciation to the Bicycle Alliance of Washington for printing a short article of mine several years ago in their newsletter, parts of which are included in this book.

CONTENTS

Knarly old tree on the pass to Satsop Lakes.

INTRODUCTION

I wrote this guidebook primarily for cross-country mountain bikers and other folks who enjoy muscle-powered recreation. In it I describe 24 routes for day trips through the national and state forests surrounding Olympic National Park. All these rides entail an ascent to a unique vista of the Olympic Mountains and the adjacent bodies of water, and/or a bumpy cruise on a single track through one of the islands of old growth forest outside the National Park. However, since most of the mileage is on old logging roads through country that was logged off in the not-so-distant past, some people venturing into these hills may be disappointed that the scenery isn't pristine. To gain insight on how to find recreation in a cutover land, here is a brief history of the Olympics and how I came to discover the trails.

For those of you who may not be familiar with the region, the Olympic Peninsula is in the northwest corner of the Washington State, and therefore at the very corner of the continental United States. Long before it received its present geopolitical description, several seafaring tribes of Native Americans called chunks of it home. They still do. Spaniards were the first Europeans to see it and they left behind cool names like Puerto de Nuestra Señora de Los Angeles, which English-speaking people truncated into Port Angeles. Under England's flag, Captain Vancouver and his crew charted the Strait of Juan de Fuca and Puget Sound in 1792 and thus determined that the clump of mountains greeting them as they sailed in from the Pacific was surrounded by water on three sides. The Indians had known that for thousands of years but the British claimed bragging rights to the discovery plus possession of everything else they laid eyes on.

After title to this real estate passed to the United States of America and the land began fragmenting into the hands of local jurisdictions and private citizens, the thick forests, rugged topography, isolation and rain made homesteading difficult and unprofitable. On the other hand, the trees were a resource for entrepreneurs to exploit. Cutting them down and sawing them into lumber provided jobs for the cash-starved immigrants. The wood was basically free for the taking, too, just as it had been in other parts of the country where forests and watersheds had already been destroyed. However, by the time the robber barons began salivating over the trees on the peninsula, resistance to cut-and-run lumbering had started to form in the eastern United States and in California. The conservation movement morphed quickly into two distinct factions: the preservationists guided by John Muir, and the "wise users" led by Gifford Pinchot.

Initially, Pinchot had more impact on the Olympic Peninsula. He was a member of a wealthy family who had made its money in lumbering on the east coast. His father, partly out of sense of guilt, suggested to Gifford that he become a forester. Gifford took up the idea but when he graduated from Yale in 1889 there were no forestry schools in the United States. In fact there were hardly any foresters either, so Pinchot went to Europe to study the field and returned in late 1890 determined to make an impact. That he did.

In 1891, Congress passed a law that allowed the president to set aside forest reserves in the public domain. President Benjamin Harrison promptly formed the first one, the Yellowstone Park Timberland Reserve of 1.25 million acres outside of Yellowstone National Park. Six years later, Pinchot and his allies got President Grover Cleveland to add another 21.3 million acres to the system, including 2,188,000 acres on the Olympic Peninsula. Next, with President Teddy Roosevelt's help, Pinchot transformed a small bureau in the Department of Agriculture into the United States Forest Service and wrestled control of the forest reserves from the Department of the Interior. The two million acres on the peninsula became the Olympic National Forest.

Pinchot was dedicated to managing the public domain for the good of all citizens, but for him that meant "making the forest pay," even if he curtailed the cut-and-run method of forestry. There was no room in his concept of management for preserving chunks of the wilderness, and—at least in the beginning—no apparent need for it either. However, over the next few decades innovations in mechanical technology made it possible to liquidate an ancient forest even as dense as the Olympic and turn it into a tree farm.

Counterbalancing the impulse to exploit our natural resources to the fullest, John Muir helped found the Sierra Club, became its first president, and lobbied presidents to form national parks. He made his living by exploring the American wilderness and writing about it. As the population expanded, became urbanized and more abstracted from the land, the popularity of his views grew. Although he died in 1914, his work continued to energize preservationists and in the 1930s, the call to form the Olympic National Park got loud. At the local level, the Port Angeles Chamber of Commerce backed the idea and hired an ex-Forest Service ranger named Chris Morgenroth to lead the effort. He drew the boundaries for the initial proposal and with others lobbied Congressman Monrad Wallgren of Everett to introduce a bill in the U.S. House of Representatives creating the Park. It didn't go anywhere at first but President Franklin Roosevelt liked the idea too. In 1938, after much politicking, he signed a bill that transferred nearly 900,000 acres from the Department of Agriculture back to the Department of the Interior for the new wilderness preserve. That still left over a million acres of timber for the Forest Service to sell and after World War II the onslaught began.

I joined the big cut in 1976. After graduating from the University of Puget Sound with a degree in English and a bone spur on my forehead from playing football, I got a job setting chokers, the entry level position in logging, for Simpson Timber Company. The company had exclusive rights to the timber in the southwestern part of the Olympic National Forest, and for the better part of eight years I considered Camp Grisdale as home. Grisdale was Simpson's logging camp on the Wynoochee River and it was the last camp in the Pacific Northwest. Some said it was the last one in the lower 48 states. As we liquidated the virgin forest, each one of us was conscious of playing a role in a part of the American West that was about to end.

In 1984 I left the woods to go back to college. A year later Simpson closed Grisdale and stopped logging old growth because the little bit left was too expensive to cut and haul to the mills. The spotted owl issue heated up not long after that and energized public debate until 1994, when President Bill Clinton signed the Northwest Forest Plan that virtually brought logging in the publicly owned coastal forests to a standstill. Old growth logging wasn't going to last much longer anyway because there weren't many of the big old trees left standing outside the national parks and wilderness areas, especially on the Olympic Peninsula.

By then, a continuous clearcut, mottled sparsely with small islands of old growth, surrounded Olympic National Park. For the majority of people, this buffer was a no-man's land. "Ruined" was a popular word to describe the land I had worked on and even loggers had to admit it was ugly. However, my comrades and I knew we hadn't destroyed it. Although we had been society's instruments for over-harvesting the forest, our proximity to the teeth of the saw allowed us to see that we did not have the power to kill it off. The woods were even greater than the stands of old trees. We were no match for the rock bones of the ridges, the rivers, the dirt, the rain and the sunlight. The so-called inanimate parts of the ecosystem contained a seed that ten thousand men with chainsaws could not stop from growing. Oddly, working on clearcuts strengthened my bond to the forest.

A few years after leaving the woods for the city, I started to return once in a while just to walk old logging operations, or logging shows as we aptly called them, and stand on stumps where I had watched cables drag logs uphill to landings. I needed to see how the land was recovering and would look at the baby trees starting to peek over the charred remains of the culls, feeling a connection to a cycle that was unfolding a lot slower than my own life. As the logging roads began to crumble, blocking my truck, I started taking a mountain bike with me and by doing so discovered that I enjoyed pedaling up the long hills and coasting back down. The views from the ridge tops and my knowledge of the roads made me realize that in most places a person on a bike could ride from one river drainage to another across large sectors of the National Forest.

The next step was to wonder if I could find a route clear around the peninsula using old logging roads. In places I realized that we would have to build connecting trails between dead ends in order to link the segments, but that didn't seem like a big deal. I began studying maps and systematically exploring a route. It took me nine years and about 60 trips to cover all the rideable segments. On most of those excursions I said to myself, "The trail is here."

Measured vertically from the bottoms of the river valleys to the crests of the divides, the route gained a total of 47,000 feet. Scaled out horizontally on U.S. Geological Survey (USGS) maps, it was nearly 400 miles long. Three hundred miles were on old logging roads in various conditions. The Forest Service and Washington State Department of Natural Resources still took care of the main lines, but well over half were double tracks the agencies had formerly decommissioned or nature was turning into single tracks.

The route also utilized fragments of hiking trails in the National Forest that survived the logging. These were perhaps the most precious segments since they wove through stands of old growth. Trails along the Quilcene, South Fork of the Skokomish and Humptulips Rivers were already open to mountain bikes. In every quadrant the route touched stands of ancient timber where people could find solitude amongst old trees. However, pedaling through the fields of saplings in the clearcuts and watching them grow into a new forest and heal the land, while contemplating my relationship with it, was the main recreational experience for me. Riding my bike onto this land and watching it recover made me feel stronger and gave me hope.

To illustrate the idea of connecting the various segments of roads and trails into a continuous path, an artist drew a map for me and entitled it the Circle Trail. I showed the map to the U.S. Forest Service, Washington State Department of Natural Resources, various bicycle clubs, and the Backcountry Horsemen of Washington. Everyone I talked to liked the idea and wanted to help make some version of the Circle Trail become a reality, but that would take a long time. Meanwhile, most of this trail already existed and there were good segments in the high country with fantastic scenery or stands of old timber big enough to get lost in, at least metaphorically.

Another attractive feature was that the routes I found were open to everyone, unlike the trails in the National Park and wilderness areas. Mountain bikers, runners, people on horses, and wheelchair athletes could use the old roads. People could even take their dogs. In some places you had to watch out for folks on quads and motorized trail bikes, but you could hear them coming from a mile away and the peaceful sounds of the woods quickly returned after they roared by. In my opinion, the addiction to speed and gasoline robbed the essence of the hills from the people riding the machines but their passage did help maintain a few of the routes. The ones who stopped and talked to me were nice people, too. Getting out on the land, exposing myself to the elements and pushing myself physically not only produced a personal connection to the environment, it also gave rise to a communal feeling.

The rides featured on the following pages will take you to vistas, lakes, waterfalls and stands of old growth that most people don't know about or have written off because they think these wild and natural features have been destroyed. I don't spend a lot of words describing them. Taking you there in your brain is not my objective. I want to tell you how to get to the places so you can go see for yourself how well the land is recovering and how beautiful it still is. Because I visit it so often, I have come to believe that wilderness can be an expanding entity and that muscling through the fringe areas around Olympic National Park on a bike or on foot allows us to participate in the changes taking place. Perhaps by using these routes more frequently, people will bond with this landscape and make it less likely that we will log it as intensely as we did in the last century. I hope this book will motivate some of you to give it a try.

Notes on Maps & Roads

If you want to study maps other than the ones I drew for this book, I suggest either a series of Forest Service maps of each ranger district on the Olympic Peninsula or the Washington State Public Land Quadrangles published by the Washington State Department of Natural Resources. The easiest way to obtain Forest Service maps is to stop at one of the many ranger stations around the peninsula and inquire at the information counter. The Forest Service maps have contour lines on them but don't include all of the roads outside of federal jurisdiction. The DNR maps, on the other hand, have all of the roads, or at least 95% of them, but no contour lines. I bought my DNR maps at Metsker Maps near the Pike Place Market in Seattle. The DNR headquarters in Forks is another good place to look at maps and check out road and trail conditions on state land.

Then of course there are the USGS maps. Those are the best but because of their scale and expense they are difficult to tote in the woods. The internet provides other options, too, like Google Earth and Mapquest. Combined with the nifty global positioning systems available on the market today, there is no reason to get lost out there. Right. Don't be that naïve. But the times you remember most may occur when you are tired, cold, wet, hungry and a little lost. If you do lose track of where you are, stay on the road or trail. Don't head off cross-country. That's my only advice.

On a related issue, every road has a number. The Forest Service identifies most of their roads by numbers with 4 digits. That is the norm. Other Forest Service roads have only 2 digits. Those are main trunk roads that are often paved and run through several drainages. Still others, minor spur roads, have 3 digits. The 2- and 4-digit road numbers are unique but the 3-digit numbers can be used several times around the peninsula. I abbreviate Forest Service roads as FS or FSR. I also follow the custom of foresters and loggers of prefacing them with "the." I do the same thing with the DNR roads, which also have 4 digits. DNR roads, though, are preceded by letters that usually indicate what river drainage they are in or what town they are close to. Most places in the field, both Forest Service and DNR roads, have a stake with the number inscribed on it at the beginning of the road. Don't count on them always being there, though.

If you don't have much experience traveling beyond the pavement, study a map and develop a picture of it in your head before setting out on a trip. Then as you ride or walk, refresh that image by looking at the map once in a while when you come to significant and recognizable features. After a while you will gain a feel for the geography and be able to maintain your location in your head. It's cheaper than buying a GPS unit and doesn't require batteries.

It is also impossible to take a snapshot of the trail conditions. Fall and winter storms wash out roads and knock down trees onto trails. Sometimes it takes years for the Forest Service or volunteers to repair the damage. Please don't blame me if you try to ride one of these routes and find that a slide or windfall makes you carry your bike through the brush for a ways, or worse, forces you to turn back. Venturing onto the land is always an adventure. Otherwise it wouldn't be any fun.

Difficulty Rating System (or Lack of One)

I don't have a formal system of rating the difficulty of these rides. This is bike riding, after all, not rock climbing. However, I usually express my perception of each trip's sweat factor. A ride is easy, hard or some simple variation of those extremes. To figure out what that means and how to relate my perceptions to your own capabilities, here are some insights into my physical condition. I'm in my 50s, stand 6′1″, weigh 240 pounds at the moment, have had a heart attack, and am in pretty good shape. Sounds like an oxymoron, doesn't it? These rides are not time trials for me. When I say a ride takes so many hours, I include intervals for getting off my bike and walking or for sitting at a viewpoint enjoying the sights.

On the other hand, most of these rides are difficult compared to ones on paved roads and bike trails. They aren't leisurely "family rides." The ridge routes I describe on the west side of the peninsula are suitable for older kids and young teenagers who enjoy and can tolerate sustained exercise.

Highly Recommended Gear

1. Bicycle with fat tires, lots of gears, good brakes and a front shock absorber
2. Tire pump
3. Extra tube and/or patch kit
4. Combination bicycle tool
5. Chain breaker and extra links
6. Spoke wrench
7. Rag
8. Rubber raincoat with hood—construction or fisherman quality
9. Bicycle helmet
10. Gloves
11. Warm shirt
12. Food and water
13. Band-aids

Safety Tips

1. Don't bother wearing a bicycle helmet while pedaling up a long hill but put it on before coasting back down.
2. Lower the seat, and your center of gravity, before making a descent.
3. Put on gloves and sun or safety glasses before zooming downhill.
4. Wear a helmet while on single track.
5. Make sure your brakes are in good shape.
6. Slow down while going around corners. I can't stress this enough, especially on roads because there are cliffs on the downhill side in many places.
7. Be courteous to people in cars or on motorbikes and ATVs, a.k.a. quads. Watch out for them, too.

Keep it on the road.

Wildflowers above the Sol Duc.

North Peninsula Rides

Highway 101 is the primary feeder to just about every road system on the Olympic Peninsula. The highway starts down in the state capital of Olympia, loops up the western shore of Hood Canal, crosses over the top of the peninsula, then hangs down the west coast all the way to Mexico. Port Angeles is like the nail in the wall holding it up. The town is also pivotal for maritime traffic. The pilots who guide big vessels in and out of Puget Sound use Port Angeles as a base. Ships from all over the world anchor in its harbor behind Ediz Hook. A ferry connects Port Angeles and the United States to the Canadian city of Victoria across the Strait of Juan de Fuca. East Indian, Thai, Mexican, Chinese, Japanese and French restaurants enhance the local cuisine and travelers from elsewhere who want to avoid the traffic hassles in Seattle can buy bicycle parts and outdoor supplies in Port Angeles, too.

From another perspective, Port Angeles sits at the end of a thickening artery of strip malls that start 14 miles to the east at Sequim. Fortunately, the urban sprawl ends immediately west of town and 101 re-enters the rural fringe of the peninsula. The highway crosses the Elwha River, winds by Lake Crescent inside Olympic National Park, then climbs a long hill into commercial timberland where it remains through the turn south to Forks and the Pacific Ocean beaches. During the height of the big cut back in the 1960s and 1970s, 101 was basically a logging road crowded with convoys of trucks hauling loads of raw wood to mills and export yards. Logging trucks still barrel down the highway but nowadays it seems as if there are just as many vehicles carrying bicycles, kayaks and surfboards.

The first rides featured in this book are immediately to the west of Lake Crescent in the heights above the Sol Duc River. In the near future, a longer regional trail will connect these rides to Port Angeles and to one another. It's called the Olympic Discovery Trail and is being developed by a group of local trail activists and Clallam County, primarily on railroad beds and power line right-of-ways. When finished in 2010, the Discovery Trail will run from Port Townsend all the way to Forks.

In the Sol Duc Valley and along the north shore of Lake Crescent, it will follow the defunct Spruce Railroad which the Army built during World War I to carry spruce logs from the forests near the ocean beaches to a mill in Port Angeles. Spruce was the best material for building aircraft frames back then. The loggers were too unruly to guarantee a steady supply, so the Army took on the job of harvesting and transporting it to the mill. Ironically, they didn't finish the railroad before the end of the war. The National Park Service converted the grade along Lake Crescent into a trail over a half century later. When the Olympic Discovery Trail is done it will interface with the routes I have found in the northwest corner of the Olympic Peninsula and give people who have ridden all the way out from Port Angeles several options for side trips into the high ground.

Headed east out of Port Angeles, the Olympic Discovery Trail isn't nearly as useful to mountain bikers. Before leaving the city limits, it does cross Ennis and Morse Creeks whose drainages encapsulate obstacles that block the Circle Trail, but from there on the gap between the Strait of Juan de Fuca and mountains gets wider and the Olympic Discovery Trail stays close to the salt water. County roads off Highway 101 lead into the hills and provide access to the rides I am about to describe. In clockwise progression starting at Port Angeles they are the Deer Park Road at the eastern edge of town, the Blue Mountain Road, the Turner Cutoff Road–Lost Mountain Road west of Sequim, the Palo Alto Road east of Sequim, and the Lords Lake Loop Road north of Quilcene, which is actually quite a ways away from the other four.

Another regional trail, the Pacific Northwest Trail, has also pushed into the northeast corner of the Olympic Peninsula. That's good news for trail enthusiasts, especially those looking for long treks. The PNT starts in the Rockies and extends west to the Pacific Ocean. It is the brainchild and creation of a man named Rod Strickland and has taken him over 30 years to develop. This trail makes landfall onto the Olympic Peninsula at the Port Townsend ferry terminal and proceeds south to Discovery Bay on the Olympic Discovery Trail. At that point, the Pacific Northwest Trail leaves the Olympic Discovery Trail, crosses Highway 101, and follows the Uncas Road, the Salmon Creek Road, the Jimmycomelately Road, and finally the Palo Alto Road into the National Forest. After crossing the Dungeness River at Dungeness Forks Campground on FS 2880 and climbing a little ways to the Gray Wolf River Trailhead, the PNT disappears beyond the realm of legal mountain biking. Ron Strickland is currently attempting to extend the other end of the trail to the East Coast.

Unfortunately I haven't yet singled out a day ride in the northeast corner of the Olympics. There is a good single track called the Gold Creek Trail in the Dungeness drainage below the Buckhorn Wilderness Area. Descriptions of that ride appear in other books but having walked portions of it I doubt I have the skill to ride much of it.

The northeast corner is best known for being in the Olympic rain shadow. By the time the prevailing southwest wind off the Pacific has pushed the weather over and around the mountains to the Dungeness drainage, the clouds have lost most of their moisture. I need to warn you though. If you are in Seattle dying for a ride in the hills and it's raining, don't drive over to the peninsula and head up one of the roads listed above expecting to stay dry. Take your raingear because the patch of blue sky in the clouds hovers almost exclusively over Sequim. That town is definitely one of the most blessed spots in western Washington.

The road beyond this washout is now a trail.

Sol Duc Loop

Map 1

Synopsis: Arduous ascent, Mt. Olympus views, descent on abandoned road

Distance: 18 miles

Elevation Gain: 2400′

Time Required: 3.5 hours

How to get there

Drive west from Port Angeles on Highway 101 past Lake Crescent. About 4.5 miles west of Fairholm at the end of the lake, turn south onto Forest Service Road 2918. The sign is across the highway from an electrical substation and the Mt. Muller trailhead. This road parallels the Park Service road to Sol Duc Hot Springs. For a short distance the two roads are so close that the thin strip of trees in between them is more like a freeway median. Although cars can't get across, people with bicycles can, which is good for those riding to or from the resort or campground at the hot springs. The 2918 crosses the Sol Duc River, then five miles from the highway it crosses a bridge over the south fork of the river. I suggest parking there. If you want a longer ride, park closer to the highway.

Description

The upper reach of the Sol Duc River has three branches. The North Fork and the main stem of the river are inside the National Park, but the South Fork is completely outside the boundary and encircled by Forest Service Roads 2918 and 2920. These two roads provide one of the best loop rides on the Olympic Peninsula. It is long, arduous, and provides tremendous views of Mt. Olympus. Another attraction is that half of the ride is on abandoned road.

I suggest traveling counterclockwise, which means going up the 2920 and down the 2918. The 2920 climbs up to the rim of the valley and the view of Mt. Olympus in fewer miles than the 2918, whereas the descent on 2918 is nine miles long and most of it is abandoned road. You don't need a grand view to distract your surrender to gravity while coasting.

There aren't any signs in the upper valley denoting the roads, so you must maintain the feeling of circling the river to keep from getting sidetracked. After parking near the bridge, at approximately 1100 feet in elevation, pedal up the 2918 for 1.5 miles, then turn right onto FS 2920. The 2920 drops quickly to the river and crosses a bridge to the northwest bank. The road veers north a little ways and doglegs through tall second growth timber that has recently been thinned. The double track then begins climbing more steeply through smaller trees toward the top of the ridge. Between 2500 and 3000 feet in elevation, the view of Mt. Olympus begins to open up. The glaciers and snowfields of its wide flanks spread over a large chunk of the horizon. The various rock peaks, small by comparison to the snow and ice fields, push toward the sky. Another high peak to the west, Mt. Tom, shares the white massif.

This view is visible for the next few miles as the road weaves along the crest of the ridge. The 2920 tops out at 3500 feet in a few places.

Toward the head of the valley, the grade switches to the northeast side of the ridge and then turns slowly to the north onto another ridge. The grade on this other ridge is gentle and makes for a pleasant side trip but don't take the roads off of it unless it is part of your plan or you have the energy to backtrack up some steep hills. The road down to the west into the Sitcum drainage, FS 29, comes out on Highway 101 a couple miles north of Forks, 25 miles away. FS 29 also retreats north off the ridge to an intersection with

The South Fork of the Sol Duc River.

101 that is five miles west of the intersection with FS 2918. The downhill leg of 29 is paved and the coast down is a blast. The Olympic Discovery Trail will someday link both ends of FS 29 to the end of the 2918, thus creating several long loop rides in this area.

To continue on the shorter ride featured here, turn off the 2920 onto the 2918 back where the ridge splits in two. As mentioned earlier, there are no signs but the intersection is distinctive because the 2918 veers upward on a steep straight grade. The last time I was up there it was partially covered with brush, too. This initial hill is only a few hundred yards long and then the road flops back over to the Sol Duc side of the ridge and one last shot of Olympus. From there on it is all downhill to the bridge where I suggested parking. A stream washed out a culvert near the bottom and the Forest Service has quit maintaining the upper part of the road. It is virtually a wide single track now, especially along the head of the valley where small slides have dumped a lot of rock onto the roadbed. People on quads and motorized dirt bikes have worn paths through the rough spots, which is good. As the road drops down into the valley, it becomes a series of smooth stretches where you can fly. Put on your helmet and have fun.

Kloshe Nanitch

Map 1

Synopsis: A long sweaty climb to an old fire lookout and ridgeline single track

Distance: 6 miles from Snider to lookout, 3 miles from lookout to Mt. Muller Trail

Elevation Gain: 2500′

Time Required: 3 hours from Snider to lookout, 1 hour from there to Mt. Muller Trail

How to get there

Drive west from Port Angeles on Highway 101 past Lake Crescent. This deep long pool of fresh water fills the bottom of a slit between ridges of the northern Olympics, and the road along the southern shore has about a hundred curves in it. Don't be impatient about getting behind a slow driver because there is probably another one around the next bend. Enjoy the view. About 9.5 miles from the lake, just past the Klahowya Campground—19 miles from Forks if you are coming from that direction—turn north into Snider. Snider is a Forest Service work camp and you can park in the compound.

Description

Kloshe Nanitch is the name of the old fire lookout atop the ridge north of Highway 101. You can drive up there but I don't suggest doing so in anything less than a midsize SUV or a pickup. The road, FS 3040, starts in the work camp and is steepest at the bottom. Pedaling all the way up will make you feel worthy of receiving the view, one of the most righteous on the Olympic Peninsula. Halfway there, the road switchbacks towards the east and begins following the building ridgeline. Looking at the thick second growth, you will notice there are no stumps from the original forest. A forest fire burned off the south side of the ridge nearly a hundred years ago.

Five miles from Snider, turn off onto the 595, a spur road that forks off the 3040 onto the south side of ridge. Kloshe Nanitch is a long mile away. By now, peek-a-boo views through the trees have given you a taste of what is to come. Finally you see the lookout at the top of a hill. The Forest Service restored the structure recently and it is painted white. The color is appropriate because this one looks like it is from Cape Cod, unlike some of the shacks they built at other vantage points.

Its perch on a rock bluff is almost as spectacular as the view. To the east is Lake Crescent, nestled erotically between the folds in the mountains. The Pacific Ocean, reflecting sunlight if the sky is clear and dappled with waves that originated on the other side of the world, is to the west. Mt. Olympus is straight ahead to the south, far enough away to appreciate its regal spread of glaciers above the rest of the landscape.

The cruise back down is a blast. You can coast it without much restraint and will only have to ride the brakes near the bottom. For a more technical descent, take the foot trail between the lookout and work camp. I haven't tried it yet so let me know how it is.

To get everything out of the elevation you have gained, though, I suggest riding further east on the trail along the ridge towards Mt. Muller. This trail starts on the south side of the road just a couple hundred feet past the lookout. It branches quickly to the right onto the leg down to Snider but you should head east instead along the top of the ridge a ways before turning around. The first part of the single track is down in the trees, smooth and fun to ride. After a mile, though, it climbs into more open ground. Marmots

Lake Crescent from the ridge near Kloshe Nanitch.

or rabbits have eaten up much of the path and I had to carry my bike a lot when above the tree line. However, the view is even better than the one from the lookout. At the top of several knolls, you can see ships steaming through the Strait of Juan de Fuca to the north, as well as Lake Crescent, Mt. Olympus, and the Pacific Ocean around the rest of the compass.

Two miles from Kloshe Nanitch, the trail on the ridge meets the Mt. Muller Trail as it comes up from Highway 101. The Mt. Muller Trail continues east along the ridge to Mt. Muller, then circles back down to the trailhead. That looks to be more of a challenge than I can handle on a mountain bike so I wish you the best of luck if you give it a go. If you want to continue the loop or have dropped a car off at the Mt. Muller Trailhead, I suggest the more direct path down hill to the highway. From there it's a 5-mile ride along the highway back to Snider. When the Olympic Discovery Trail is finished in 2010, we will be able to ride most of the way back to Snider off the highway.

At the junction of trails on the ridge, another short leg drops down to the remnants of the 3040, which at one time ran from Snider all the way along the north side of the ridge and then down to State Route 112 by the Strait of Juan de Fuca. Just recently, however, the Forest Service decommissioned the middle segment of the road along the north side of the ridge. I imagine people on quads and motorized dirt bikes will eventually wear a trail that we can also use along the old grade.

N3 Pyramid Mountain

Map 1

Synopsis: A new high elevation single track with big views and backward slant

Distance: 6 miles one way

Elevation Gain: 1000′

Time Required: 4 hours round trip

How to get there

Four miles west of Port Angeles on Highway 101, turn right onto State Route 112 which runs along the Strait of Juan de Fuca all the way to Neah Bay. Proceed through the community of Joyce, 10 miles from the turnoff. Eight miles past Joyce, turn south onto Forest Service Road 3040, or the Twin River Road as it is called. Stay on the 3040 all the way to the end of the road and park at the trailhead about 10 miles from SR 112.

Description

Lake Crescent sits just inside the northernmost enclave of Olympic National Park and virgin forest blankets the slopes of the ridges on both sides of the freshwater fjord. On a map, Crescent looks like a stretched-out sea horse. Located just behind the neck of this creature on the north shore, Pyramid Mountain dominates the east end of the lake. The formation is actually the pinched-up end of the ridge that stretches 20 miles west and includes Mt. Muller and Kloshe Nanitch, featured in the previous ride. Although there is a trail from the lake to the summit, the route is in the National Park and off-limits to mountain bikers. However, an old road, the 3068, used to traverse the north side of the ridge almost all the way to the top of Pyramid and the Forest Service has just recently finished removing most of the grade and replacing it with a trail.

The ride begins by climbing a few hundred feet to 3300 feet in elevation, which is the high point for this trip. This first pitch is too steep for me to ride up but it's only about a half mile long. Beyond there, the route descends 1000 feet in 5 miles to the end of the trail. Just about anyone who has ridden any single track will be able to stay on their bike except where trees have fallen across the trail or rocks and dirt have slid onto it. It's amazing to see how this brand-new trail has already started to decay. Not that the Forest Service did a lousy job. On the contrary. They didn't simply pull the culverts out and abandon the old road, but actually dug it up and removed or reshaped the road ballast into more natural contours. Therefore, the wide trail on top of the new earthwork dips along the landscape like trails are supposed to and riding it out to Pyramid Mountain is a lot of fun. In a way it's like an addictive drug. As the trail slowly drops you know that you are going to have to climb back up, but it pulls you along and you cannot stop. The scenery is spectacular, too. Several north-facing overlooks provide views of the Strait of Juan de Fuca and Vancouver Island. Big ships steaming in or out of the strait look like tiny toys. Mount Baker floats on the far horizon.

Towards the end, the trail falls rather steeply for a ways then flattens out and traverses a low spot in the ridge. Pyramid Mountain is the next high point. The hiking trail to the top interfaces with the new single track at the saddle. Hopefully the Forest Service has put a sign there pointing out the path to the top of the mountain. I missed it and pedaled the next half-mile to the end of the trail, where by the way there is a nice little place to camp on an old landing in the second growth. I compounded my mistake by hiking up to the top of Pyramid through the woods off-trail. I was already tired and climbing straight up put me into a deeper stage of exhaustion. The woods were beautiful, though, and there was a cabin on top. Time had vandalized the small structure but the roof was still intact. The old lookout was perched on the very top of the rock knob but trees obscured the panorama. The lake was visible through wide gaps in the trees.

As hinted at earlier, the 6-mile trip back to the car is a tough one since most of it is uphill, however slight the grade. Carry lots of water because there are no streams, and take plenty of energy food.

A ship in the Straits of Juan de Fuca.

N4 McDonald Mountain

Map 2

Synopsis: Short and sweet, this ride has it all

Distance: 7 miles round trip

Elevation Gain: 900'

Time Required: 2 to 3 hours

How to get there

This little exploration is directly behind Port Angeles. The easiest way to find it when entering Port Angeles from the east is to turn left (south) off Front Street, the one-way avenue Highway 101 morphs into when approaching downtown Port Angeles, onto Hurricane Ridge Road (also known as Race Street). Drive uphill past the National Park headquarters and visitor center all the way to Heart O' the Hills. Just before the tollbooth at Heart O' the Hills, turn right, or west, towards Lake Dawn on the Little River Road. Drive west on the Little River Road for 3 miles and park at the Little River trailhead. The trailhead is next to the intersection of Little River Road and Black Diamond Road, which also provides a more direct route to and from Port Angeles for those who know the area. Another way, if you're driving east from Forks or Lake Crescent, is to turn south off Highway 101 onto Olympic Hot Springs Road where the main highway crosses the bridge over the Elwha River. Then turn again almost immediately onto Little River Road and proceed east a few miles to the end of the pavement and the trailhead.

A note here: You can also ride into Olympic Hot Springs, which is inside Olympic National Park and slightly beyond the scope of this book. A resort once monopolized this natural resource but now only several spa-sized natural pools of hot water scattered amongst the trees are left. Sitting in them is very pleasant but I prefer going up there in winter when it's snowy and I have to walk or ski.

Description

I like the ride up McDonald Mountain for the variety of trails and roads it utilizes. It also ventures into a fringe area on the edge of the National Park that not many people visit. It's a fairly short trip and starts out from the Little River Trailhead by dipping down over the aptly named stream, then rising back to a bench at the bottom of the mountains. I had to walk my bike up the sides of the gully. Shortly past the ravine, another trail veers to the west. That's the way to McDonald Mountain but I suggest you first ride the Little River Trail to the boundary of the National Park about a mile away. The relatively flat single track is too nice a ride to pass up. At the boundary, the trail contacts the South Branch of Little River and starts climbing towards Hurricane Ridge. You aren't supposed to ride into the National Park, but since you are there you should get off your bike and walk in a little ways to see the old growth and cascading stream.

Back on your bike, head towards the trailhead then turn onto the other trail mentioned above. This is a short spur that leads out to Forest Service Road 3030. Turn left there. The 3030 is gated out by the Little River Road so there should be no traffic. Traveling roughly southwest, it drops down to the South Branch and ends at a garage-like structure, the inlet and treatment facility for a local water system. The road resumes on the other side of the stream and from there on it's unofficially reserved for people who like to sweat. If you don't want to get your feet wet, there is a walk log across the stream in back of the building. No matter how you get across, be respectful to the water because other people may soon be drinking it.

For about two and half miles, the 3030 climbs up the side of McDonald Mountain, which forms the eastern side of the notch through which the Elwha River flows out of the National Park and mountains. It has been a while since logging trucks have driven up this road but foot traffic, mountain bikers, and animals have begun establishing a single track on the grade. The second growth along the lower stretches is thick and tall. Better yet, the route goes through some nice stands of low-elevation old growth. The grade gets steeper and then enters newer clearcuts that open up views to the west and north. By the time the road ends at a landing high on the mountain, you can see north through the outer notch in the foothills to the Strait of Juan de Fuca.

If you're in the mood, leave your bike there and hike up what looks like an old fire trail into the old growth at the top of the ridge. That's at the edge of the National Park and I don't suggest going beyond there unless you are an experienced woodsman or woman and know how to keep from getting permanently lost. Go up and have a look though. It's like peering into deep water while snorkeling along the edge of a reef. The ride back down the road is short but sweet.

The South Branch of Little River.

Slab Camp Road

Map 3

Synopsis: Single track so blissful you'll tip your hat to the folks straddling gas engines who keep it open

Distance: 10 miles one way

Elevation Gain: 600′

Time Required: 3 hours one way

How to get there

This ride can be accessed from four different spots. To get to the west end, closest to Port Angeles, turn south off Highway 101 onto Deer Park Road. This road is easy to find since it intersects 101 at the movie theater complex at the very eastern, and ever-expanding, edge of Port Angeles. Drive all the way up Deer Park Road to the boundary of Olympic National Park, where a large pile of dirt blocks the entrance to a side road heading east. That's the start of Slab Camp Road.

To reach the east end, turn south off Highway 101 just past Sequim onto Taylor Cutoff Road on the west side of the bridge over the Dungeness River. At the end of Taylor Cutoff, take Lost Mountain Road. After about 3 miles where it comes down a hill and starts to bend to the west, turn south onto Forest Service Road 2870. Less than a mile after that, turn right onto Forest Service Road 2875 and drive up the hill a few more miles to Slab Camp, which is a small campground. If you want an extra treat, drive or ride from Slab Camp a couple of miles further out the 2875 to an overlook of the Buckhorn Wilderness Area and the 7,000-foot peaks along Gray Wolf Ridge. Since this is on the dry side of the Olympics, the view might make you think you are in the Rockies.

You can also access Slab Camp Road at two intermediate points near the end of Blue Mountain Road. Entering this trail at one of these spots might be a good idea because of the segmented nature of the trail. Parking at one end and riding to the other end and back is a big commitment.

Description

Finding and exploring what I call Slab Camp Road was one of my most satisfying achievements since it filled a considerable gap in the Circle Trail outside of the National Forest. It utilizes one of the oldest—and almost forgotten—roads on the periphery of the Olympic Mountains. It's so old that it is hardly there anymore. Fortunately the local horse riders, dirt bikers, quad enthusiasts, mountain bikers, and walkers have kept this travel corridor alive. It's not totally continuous since the westernmost segment goes through a privately owned section of land that has been subdivided into large estates. The roads through there—Marmot Loop, the end of the Blue Mountain Road, and High Country Drive—are public and the smooth, even surfaces give a person like me a welcome respite from the pounding out on the trail.

I think of this trail as starting at the west end on Deer Park Road, at the edge of both the National Park and an old clearcut outside the boundary. There is plenty of space to park beside the mound of dirt that blocks the old logging road. On the other side of the obstacle, the trail on the old road goes straight for a couple hundred yards past some turnoffs, then takes a turn to the south and drops into the National Park. It may be a little confusing but try to stay on the most beaten path and keep in mind that you are going to turn south into the National Park. Once under the tree canopy, the path evolves more into a single track, turns east, and parallels the boundary for almost a mile just inside the federal wilderness reserve. In a couple of spots people on quads and motorbikes have beaten the trail around skeletons of old log bridges. You will also begin to appreciate why the folks on motorized equipment often carry chainsaws with them, although there are a couple of spots where you will wish you could help them cut a few more windfalls out of the way. Generally though, the relatively flat and smooth stretches of this section are a blast to ride. The mud holes are fun, too.

The trail crosses back into state land but the character of the ride doesn't change until it rises to a locked gate, enters a new clearcut, comes to the end of the Marmot Loop Road, and enters the developed land I mention above. Follow Marmot to Blue Mountain Road, take a left, which is counter-intuitive, then take a right onto High Country Drive. High Country proceeds straight and true along the section line for a mile. Near the end it veers slightly to the right, or south, into a llama farm. Immediately before that change in direction, turn right onto an abandoned road that veers more sharply to the south. Having returned to what I call the Slab Camp Road, the trail on this abandoned grade skirts private property for a little ways, goes through a clearcut, then drops back into the woods.

Because this ground hasn't been logged in a long time, the second growth forest feels surprisingly deep. The trail is funky, too. The eastern part of the Slab Camp Road, which I am describing now, gets more motorized traffic than the western section. Consequently, there is more bare dirt and mud. Environmentally that may be a little stressful but sticking to the multi-use spirit of this book, the impact for mountain bikers is mostly beneficial. Staying on a bike is still a workout and here and there, where the motorized crowd hasn't bothered to saw out the windfalls, there are little detours through the brush that provide technical challenges for us sweat hogs.

A little more than a mile from High Country Drive, the Slab Camp Road

Splintered windfall on Slab Camp Road.

comes to an intersection. Stay to the right. The trail goes past a huge tank trap and transitions onto the 050 spur off Forest Service Road 2877. There are no road markers in here and if you miss the 050 don't worry. The other leg of the intersection runs over to the end of the Lost Mountain Road and if you find yourself there, simply turn around and come back. A local couple on dirt bikes also turned me onto another, unmapped spur between the leg to Texas Valley and Forest Service Road 2875. That spur climbed over a steep hill and allowed me to ride a loop back to my pickup near Slab Camp.

Mud on the Slab Camp Road.

However, for simplicity the first time you venture into the area I suggest staying on the 050. It is very muddy down at the bottom and you will notice it is a little wider than the trail you have been riding so far. That is because jeepers and other maniacs drive their 4x4s down the hill from the Forest Service roads and Slab Camp. Some don't make it out as illustrated by an abandoned S-10 in a mud hole. The windows have been broken out, parts cannibalized, and the vehicle is just scrap metal now as far as I can tell. At least people can carry mountain bikes out, as long as they can still walk. I actually pushed my bike part way up the hill to the 2877 the last time I was there, more for the change of pace than anything else. It was quiet, too. I couldn't hear any gas engines. Following the tire tracks back down the hill was a lot of fun.

There is no particular reason to go all the way to Slab Camp other than it makes a good rallying point and you may decide to camp there. There are two other larger campgrounds in the vicinity down on the Dungeness River a short drive away.

The Eastern Front

I have a difficult time thinking of the eastern slopes of the Olympics as east because I am always looking west at them from Seattle. These peaks have inspired me all my life. Geologically, they are the teeth on the serrated edge of a shield volcano that the continental shelf scraped off the ocean floor and stood on edge. All along the front range, bare mounds of pillow basalt buttress the mountains. The slab of rock wraps around most prominently to the north where it slowly recedes back under the ground, thus forming the Olympic Crescent. Along the eastern rim, the formation sketches out a jagged line in the sky that I look for to know that I am home.

The flanks of the mountains and their narrow band of foothills rise steeply out of Hood Canal, the other prominent feature of the geography. This straight ditch off Puget Sound drains the full length of mountains, then hooks back north and east a short ways before ending. Highway 101 hugs the shoreline between the water and the hills. County roads in the lower valleys of the rivers that drain into the Canal provide avenues to the strip of Forest Service land buffering the National Park. These paved arteries become dirt roads well before they reach the Park, then branch out laterally into the hills that sit in front of the mountains.

A network of old logging roads straddles the ridges between the five major streams flowing out of the Olympics into Hood Canal. Starting in the north, these are the Quilcene, Dosewallips, Duckabush, Hamma Hamma, and Skokomish Rivers. Two small towns, Quilcene and Hoodsport, sit like bookends to the series of river valleys. Technically, Hoodsport to the south is north of the mouth of the Skokomish, but the road up to

Lake Cushman—on the North Fork of that river—starts in the center of town. Both burgs are also close to developing population pressure points. Port Townsend is about 25 miles north of Quilcene and Shelton is 16 miles south of Hoodsport, but neither of the smaller communities has a stoplight, a McDonald's, or a Starbucks Coffee joint. The stretch of Highway 101 between the little towns feels even more remote and idyllic as it winds along the salt chuck. The deltas are especially poetic. Tree trunks, mineral aggregate and spawned-out salmon, torn and washed out of the mountains by the forces of nature and chunks of beauty in their own right, lie in the grassy estuaries and mudflats, waiting for the tides to spread them further along the shoreline. It is always a struggle not to slow down and back up traffic to gawk at the scenery when heading to the woods. Perhaps when my legs can no longer carry me up the hills I will settle closer to the mud at the mouth of one of these rivers.

My favorite hill climb on a bike in the Olympics, the one I call The Brothers, starts at the upper Duckabush bridge. The Hamma Hamma is the best drainage for strenuous day hikes on this side of the Olympics. The Lena Lakes, Mildred Lake, and Skyline Trails all provide quick access to the high country. The trail to Lower Lena is also open to mountain biking. However, because it is not on or adjacent to the Circle Trail and because of its rich tradition with hikers, I have no desire to include it on my list of best mountain bike rides. I have had too much success and fun discovering routes on marginal paths that take people into areas that are on the mend. On the Hamma Hamma, the ride up to Elk Lake and beyond provides you with an opportunity to observe the fusion between clearcut recovery and chunks of the old growth forest that avoided the chainsaw, all while experiencing aerobic exercise.

There are two excellent, low-key Forest Service campgrounds on the Hamma Hamma and the Forest Service rents out the ranger house at the old guard station. They do the same with the Interrorem Guard Station on the Duckabush. Collins Campground, another smaller, less developed spot to car camp, is upstream from there. In fact there are at least 12 formal campgrounds, run by various agencies, on Hood Canal and the rivers between Quilcene and Potlatch, just south of Hoodsport. While riding and driving the dirt roads, you will also find a multitude of other fire circles on side streams, lakes, ponds, and old logging landings with great views. On nice weekends in summer, the hills may seem a little crowded, but the rest of the time they are relatively empty.

While exploring a route for the Circle Trail along the eastern edge of the peninsula, I was unable to find existing roads and trails across all the ridges between the rivers. Describing or proposing projects to close these gaps goes beyond the scope of this guidebook. But if you like the idea of creating a continuous route around the Olympics for muscle-powered recreation and want to help, please keep an ear open. I imagine volunteers will do a lot of the work. In the meantime, I must point out that the Forest Service does have a road that skirts the high country all the way from the Duckabush to Lake Cushman. I call it the "low road," and have driven it many times. However, as you can tell by now, I prefer pedaling my bike into the high ground where I can see long distances and then coast back down a big hill. Therefore, the short rides I describe—as well as the travel corridor I have found through the area—remain faithful to the vertical inclination of the topography as seen from Seattle.

The Brothers and Mt. Jupiter.

Quilcene River

Maps 4 & 5

Synopsis: Gentle sloping single track through trees, an Olympic Peninsula favorite

Distance: 14 miles round trip

Elevation Gain: 1500'

Time Estimate: 3-4 hours

How to get there

Drive to the town of Quilcene on Highway 101 and continue south. Stop at the Quilcene Ranger Station for a Trail Park Pass if you haven't got one. A mile or so further, turn right onto the Big Quilcene River Road. Follow it up 4 miles out of the second growth forest to the top of a knoll. That is a good place to park but you might also want to turn right onto Forest Service Road 27. Shortly thereafter turn left to the official lower parking lot and trailhead. It's also possible to park at the upper trailhead. To get there, keep driving 5 miles up the 27 to the 2750, turn left and drive another 4 miles over to the trailhead.

Description

With parking lots at both the high and low ends, there are several different ways to do the Quilcene Trail. Being a punishment/reward kind of guy, I

Young Sean Yancey ripping down the Quilcene Trail.

prefer to park at the bottom. If you're a real glutton, you can park all the way back at Quilcene. But when you get up near the lower trailhead, you still have to decide whether to pedal up the road and come down the trail, or ride your bike both up and down the trail. In this case, I prefer to pedal up the road, which is a lot easier for me than riding up a single track.

Road 27 is also one of the logging roads that the Forest Service paved a long time ago and it's a smooth ride no matter what direction you are traveling. Therefore rolling resistance is minimal and you'll think you are on a highway, only there will be little or no traffic. It's a long 5 miles and 1300 feet in elevation to the turnoff onto the 2750 road, then another 4 miles over various grades to the upper trailhead, 200 feet higher than the crossroads. From there, the lower parking lot is about 5 trail miles and 1500 vertical feet below.

Technically, the trail isn't very difficult so it's perfect for the likes of me. The first mile where the trail descends to the Big Quilcene River is on the steepest grade and even that is not very severe. Once it begins following the stream the grade flattens out and allows you to pick up some speed if you want. An old campsite called Camp Jolley, an excellent spot for a picnic or overnight camping, is about halfway down. Below there, the big trees thin out and the trail eventually widens into the decayed remnant of an old road. There is plenty of room to pass hikers but please be courteous and slow way down when you see one. If your car is at the lower parking lot, perhaps you can talk someone in your party to drive it to Quilcene because it's all downhill and that coast is a lot of fun, too.

Mt. Turner Loop

Map 5

Synopsis: A nice aerobic loop on double track perched above Hood Canal

Distance: 10 miles

Elevation Gain: 1500′

Time Required: 2.5 hours

How to get there

At the top of Walker Pass 4 miles south of Quilcene, turn west off Highway 101 onto Rocky Brook Road (Forest Service Road 2620), and drive up the steep grade to Rocky Brook Pass. Stay on the main road and drop down 2.5 miles on the other side to the second intersection you come to. Park there. The road veering off to the southeast is the 030 spur. If you are coming from the south, turn off 101 at Brinnon onto the Dosewallips Road. Turn right at the top of a hill a mile later onto the south end of Rocky Brook Road. The intersection with the 030 spur is 3.75 miles uphill from there.

Description

As you'll see from the litter of beer cans and shell casings around the remnants of bonfires, Rocky Brook Pass appears to be a place where the local teenagers like to party. Doesn't sound like an appealing spot, does it? But as a link between the Quilcene and Dosewallips Rivers, it has strategic

Gordy Yancey grinding up the pass near Mt. Turner.

importance to the Circle Trail. In addition, several old logging roads—all good bike rides—fan out from there like butterfly wings to the high points along the ridge. Every turn in the road reveals a new perspective of the higher mountains or Hood Canal below.

The 030 spur around Mt. Turner provides the only smooth and continuous loop ride in the area, and it's a good one. This road connects onto Rocky Brook Road at the first two intersections south of Rocky Brook Pass and you can park about anywhere. If you are like me and prefer to end rides with fast plunges, park at the lower intersection and ride counterclockwise. The first 3 miles of this ride are basically level through pleasant maturing second growth forest more characteristic of the lower elevations of the National Forest rather than the 2000-foot level. As the road swings to the north you get the feeling of being perched above Hood Canal even though it's not always visible through the trees. Three miles from the start, at the intersection of another spur road that rises nearly to the top of Mt. Turner, the 030 dips down a little then begins to climb. I imagine the road up Mt. Turner is a good side trip but when I made this ride I didn't think I had enough time for the diversion. The 030 provided enough of a workout for me. Over the next 3.75 miles it rises 1500 feet to a pass nearly a thousand feet higher than Rocky Brook Pass and probably higher than Mt. Turner as well. Great views of Hood Canal and the Puget Sound Basin begin to open up as you near the top of the pass. At the summit you will get a great panorama of the Olympic front range.

The rest of the ride back to the car is all downhill. It's about a mile and a quarter to the upper intersection with the Rocky Brook Road, then 2 miles further to the lower intersection. Have fun and be safe.

The Brothers

Map 5

Synopsis: Best grueling hill climb on the Olympic Peninsula

Distance: 9 miles each way

Elevation Gain: 3600′

Time Required: 3.5 hours up, 45 minutes down

How to get there

Along Hood Canal, south of Brinnon, turn off Highway 101 onto the Duckabush River Road. Drive upstream beyond the pavement into the National Forest. Pass the Interrorem Guard Station (which you can rent from the Forest Service), Collins Campground (which I recommend), the trailhead, and cross the bridge. Immediately thereafter, park at one of the wide spots near the intersection with Forest Service Road 2530.

Description

Being open to vehicle traffic is this route's only shortcoming but since it dead-ends at the top, don't expect to see many cars or trucks. The views that unfold while climbing the 3600 feet make it an exquisite ride. Even the second growth forest at the bottom of the valley is good to look at. The Forest Service has cultivated these trees into a fledgling old growth forest.

Mt. Constance from the road to Trap Pass.

They thinned it out decades ago. The trees, probably 80 years old or so, are getting big, and an under story is growing up. This is the way all our cutover public land on the peninsula should be managed. We should let these stands grow 150 to 200 years before cutting them down. Enough preaching. A mile or so from the bottom, a side trail over to Murhut Falls makes for a nice diversion. However, if you are like me, by that point you will be warmed up and have a good rhythm going that will be difficult to interrupt. I haven't seen Murhut Falls yet but several people who have assure me that it's worth the extra sweat. Someday I'll get over there.

The trees gradually get smaller and at a bend in the road a view up the Duckabush Valley into The Brothers Wilderness Area opens up. This first vista is unmarred by signs of human development. The expanse increases with every contour line you reach: first Mt. Jupiter to the north, and then Mt. Constance beyond that. Towards the head of the side valley the grade eases off and actually drops for a ways, then—where Murhut Creek tumbles out of a stand of old growth—it turns nearly 180 degrees and begins climbing in the other direction. Near the end of this next long switchback, you start getting looks down the Duckabush at Hood Canal, Puget Sound and the Cascade Mountains in the far distance. After turning back to the south one last time, the road keeps climbing and Mt. Rainier emerges above the hazy smog covering the megalopolis along the Sound. Trap Pass sits in the crosshairs between the handlebars and when you reach it the Olympic front range south of The Brothers—Mt. Washington in particular—suddenly takes over the foreground.

Don't stop. At the top of the pass, the road turns to the west, dips slightly to another saddle, then swings back to the south. From there it climbs through a stand of intact trees where a slide has blocked motor vehicles. A little ways further the road turns to the west and at that spot you find yourself staring at The Brothers, the twin-peaked mountain at the center of Olympic skyline as seen from Seattle. You don't need to go any further because the road descends steeply to its end. But if you have any energy left, go back a short ways to that last stand of timber, park your bike, and scramble up through the trees to a rock knob on the top of the ridge. There's room for a few people to sit and if the air is clear enough you'll be able to see the skyscrapers in Seattle. And just think, when you return to your bike you have all that vertical to descend! There's so much of it you might even get tired of going fast.

High elevation forest.

Elk Lake, Washington Pass

Map 6

Synopsis: Combo of funky old trail and roads, with options

Distance: 6 miles one way

Elevation Gain: 1000′

Time Required: 2 hours up

How to get there

North of Hoodsport and 2 miles north of the highway bridge over the Hamma Hamma River, turn west off Highway 101 onto the Hamma Hamma River Road. About 6 miles later, just past the Hamma Hamma Campground, turn left onto FS 2480 and cross the bridge. Proceed a quarter mile downstream, then turn right onto the first road you come to, FS 2421. A mile and a quarter up the hill, the 2421 turns sharply to the west. Park there. The trail to Elk Lake begins at the elbow of the road. For a longer ride with a little more vertical, park by the bridge.

Description

This ride mixes a little single track, road climb, and fast descent with some nice territorial scenery. The initial segment of the route follows the Elk Lake

Trail, which is in old growth. The single track traverses the steep sidehill above Jefferson Creek and there are several spots where riding off the downhill side could be hazardous, if not fatal. The path also goes through a patch of madrona trees, which is unusual because they normally grow down by the salt water. On the other hand, the old growth forest never fails to amaze me. This stand of survivors extends all the way up to and around the lower Elk Lake. A fork of the trail crosses a footbridge to an intermediate trailhead at the outlet of the lake, but I recommend squeezing all you can out of the single track and following the leg along the west side of the lake. The trees in the clearcuts on the hills to the east have grown large enough to fill the background with green. Ducks, geese, otters and beavers may be swimming across the open or scooting through the cattails along the perimeters of the lake. Watching the various images of this scene framed between the trunks of old growth trees moving with your angle of perception will add to the challenge of staying on a bike. A quarter mile past the water, the trail meets road FS 2401 and ends.

If you want, continue to ride up the road alongside Jefferson Creek to Jefferson Lake. It's bigger than Elk Lake but is also more exposed to the road due to the logging and I suppose it will be several more years before the new trees begin to hide it. A lot of people drive up this road so you probably won't have it to yourself and if it's a hot dry day you'll be eating dust. Past Jefferson Lake the 2401 begins climbing more steeply, splits in two, and fizzles out on the tops of opposing ridges. The branch to the west goes by the north abutment of Mount Washington, which is worth seeing.

However, where the Elk Lake Trail dumps out onto the road, this ride turns left, or downstream, on the 2401. A half-mile from there, turn right, or east, onto the 2441, which follows Washington Creek to Washington Pass. First, you will pass Upper Elk Lake which is right on the road and not on all maps. Then you'll climb 1000 feet in 4 miles to the top of the pass. There is nothing overly distinctive about this climb other than some good aerobic exercise and the fun descent it provides.

For a bigger ride you might want to turn onto the 2469, which veers to the left, or west, about a mile before reaching the pass. The 2469 climbs to the top of the ridge between Jefferson Creek and Hood Canal, then follows the ridge back several miles to its northern end above the Hamma Hamma.

I haven't tried this variation yet and am guessing the views of the mountains and the canal are pretty good from up there.

It is possible to ride over the pass all the way to Lake Cushman, or even to the Humptulips River if you have a few days. On the other side of the pass you can also return to the Hamma Hamma via Forest Service Roads 24 and 2480, which I call the "low road" as mentioned in the introduction to these east side rides. If you do that, though, you won't get to ride back down the Elk Lake Trail to your car, which in my opinion is the better alternative.

Twisted madrona along the Elk Lake Trail.

Dry Creek

Map 7

Synopsis: Single track ascent into big timber

Distance: 14 miles round trip

Elevation Gain: 2300′

Time Required: 3 hours

How to get there

In the middle of Hoodsport, turn off Highway 101 onto Lake Cushman Road. Proceed past the lower end of the lake to Forest Service Road 24, then turn left to Staircase. There should be plenty of signs. The Staircase River is another name for the North Fork of the Skokomish River above Lake Cushman and the Park Service runs a ranger station and campground near its mouth into the lake. At the upstream end of the lake, and downstream from the campground, take a left and cross the bridge spanning the mouth of the river. Park at the trailhead on the other side.

Description

Lake Cushman was one of the first recreational centers in the Olympic Mountains. The City of Tacoma destroyed the original tourist trade when they constructed a dam and raised the water level. Since then, state and federal agencies, with Tacoma's help, have built and maintained excellent boating, camping, and hiking facilities on or around the water. The hills and woods surrounding the lake also provide many opportunities for mountain bikers.

The Dry Creek Trail is probably the most adventurous ride in the area since it is entirely on single track on the roadless side of the lake. It is also the first of a long string of single tracks that you can ride from Cushman to the Humptulips River. Someday, with a little work, this larger trail might go all the way to Lake Quinault. How cool would that be? But even today, pieced together with the rides I describe in the next section, the Dry Creek Trail can be the start of a much longer trip.

From the trailhead, ride south along the lake. The trail starts off as a road but soon turns into single track. The first part serves a string of shoreline cabins but those soon peter out. A couple of rock outcroppings force you to get off and carry your bike a few steps but beyond those the trail has a lot of continuity. A mile and a half or so later you will come to a junction with the remnants of an old road and another trail that goes down to the lake. This ride follows the roadbed uphill but you may want to go down to the water for a swim on the way back.

The old road, which is now a trail, heads straight up Dry Creek's side valley. When I did it, there were a few easy obstacles to get around and I was able to stay on my bike for quite a ways, which was a pleasant surprise. Coming down of course was even more fun. It's almost 2 miles in a straight line up to where the trail bends and crosses the stream. There used to be a bridge but a storm washed that out years ago so, depending on the time of year, you might have to get your feet wet to go any further.

On the other side of the stream, the trail becomes a true single track and is more difficult to ride. The thick second growth forest also gives way to old growth. If you are like me, the sight of the first big trees will inspire you to keep going. Unfortunately, I left my bike there and hiked. A half-mile up hill the grade slacks off and I think I could have pedaled the rest of the way to the pass. The single track was smooth and I know I could have coasted down. However, walking up there was worth the effort. Near the top, the trail emerges into a stand of magnificent and peaceful Douglas fir.

On the other side of the pass, the trail joins up with some roads and drops down to the Skokomish River. From there the alternatives are almost unlimited.

The Southern Underbelly

Because I spent nine years working in the woods along the southern perimeter of Olympic National Park, I am biased about that part of the peninsula. It is soggy down there, cloudy most of the time, a long ways from town, and many men I worked with never wanted to see it again after liberating themselves from the logging shows. For me it had the opposite effect. I couldn't keep from going back. That is where this odyssey started, in the aftermath of my logging days.

Objectively, this "southern underbelly" provides more opportunities for technical riding than the other three sides. Most of the mileage described below is on single track in old growth. These rides can also be linked together in a longer, multi-day trek west from Lake Cushman to the top of the ridge above Lake Quinault. If we were to build a trail someday between Quinault Ridge and a Forest Service road in Wright Canyon, a side valley off the east side of Lake Quinault, we could ride all the way across to the western lake.

The hills between Cushman and Quinault are big and empty. I feel as if I have just scratched the surface of their potential for bicycling. As with everywhere else in the logged-off land surrounding the National Park, decaying roads lead to views on top of peaks and ridges that I will never see, and to old timber tucked away in forgotten valleys too numerous for me to explore. However, my feeling of incompletion is greatest down south. For example, I have yet to try biking to Pine Lake, the destination of an abandoned road near the end of the Skokomish River's South Fork. I took more trips in that area searching for the best route over the ridge into the

Satsop drainage than to any other single location and still haven't completely finished the job. Although I have settled on the travel corridor up Church Creek and over a pass to the Satsop Lakes, there is one short segment of the trail I have yet to roll my tires on. And what about the Humptulips? The trail along the west fork of that river is 16 miles long through thick ancient timber. I have taken three rides into this stretch of jungle and still haven't done the whole thing.

There are three main roads into the southern hills. The Skokomish River Road provides access to the southeastern corner. It takes off from Highway 101 seven miles north of Shelton and nine miles south of Hoodsport. Being close to Olympia, Bremerton, and the summer playgrounds on Hood Canal, the rides on the Skokomish are good day trips plus there are lots of camping spots in the upper valley if you want to spend the night. I don't recommend staying at the Brown Creek Campground, though. Too many slobs have left their beer cans and other garbage in the fire pits and hacked on the vegetation with axes. Look for informal fire rings to the sides of roads. They're all over the place and often more secluded and charming.

The road up the Wynoochee River is the second main access route. It is practically on the centerline of the peninsula and starts on the west side of Montesano. Once on the Wynoochee Road you don't have to turn off until you get to Lake Wynoochee, 35 miles away. It seems a lot further, though, because about half of it is on gravel. We used to call the unimproved portion the "camp road" because Grisdale, the logging camp where I lived and worked, was a mile inside the National Forest and another mile from the turnoff over to the dam and lake. Simpson Timber Company tore down the camp after abandoning it in 1985 and now the place is just a field of young trees. Since then Simpson has also cut down the second growth along the camp road so visually I feel lost when driving up there. The road itself hasn't changed much, though. It is wide, fairly straight, and back in the day we would average over 50 mph when cruising in or out. It takes me about three hours to drive all the way to the upper Wynoochee from Seattle. If you've never done it, allow three and a half or four hours. When you see the first big old growth trees looming above the smaller ones, you will know you are almost there.

Third, the Donkey Creek Road provides access into the southwestern corner. From Highway 101, it takes off 24 miles north of Hoquiam, three miles north of the Humptulips Store, and 15 miles south of Lake Quinault. This road is paved and runs deep into the woods. Where it swings to the east, and transitions into FS Road 22, take the turnoff north onto FS 2204 to the West Fork of the Humptulips River. Much more of the original forest remains intact on both forks in the upper watershed than in any other drainage outside the Park on the peninsula. One of the best campgrounds on the peninsula, the Campbell Tree Grove, is also located near the end of the West Fork, but be warned that it is a long ways in and there are no hot showers. The trail to the top of a mountain named Colonel Bob in the Colonel Bob Wilderness starts nearby and is an excellent day hike. In fact it continues down the other side to the Quinault, a route that I hope a bike trail will someday parallel over Quinault Ridge outside the wilderness area.

For those of you who enjoy driving adventures and can handle getting lost, I'll also point out that it is possible to drive across the southern Olympics from the Skokomish to the Humptulips. Between the Wynoochee and Donkey Creek it's a piece of cake because FS 22, the road you want to take, is a paved one-laner with turnouts. However, between the Wynoochee and the Skokomish the road is rough, steep, sometimes blocked by slides, and there are lots of turnoffs. If you want to give it a try, I suggest you study the Forest Service maps I talk about at the beginning of this book, and call the Forest Service to see if these roads are even open.

Sequestered CO_2.

LeBar Ridge Loop

Map 7

Synopsis: Strenuous uphill on road and long gradual descent on decommissioned road

Distance: 7.5 miles

Elevation Gain: 1800′

Time Required: 3.5 hours

How to get there

Nine miles south of Hoodsport and seven miles north of Shelton, turn west off of Highway 101 onto the Skokomish River Road at the George Adams Hatchery. Drive up the valley approximately eight miles and turn uphill onto Forest Service Road 23. You can also follow the signs to Brown Creek Campground. The first three miles are bumpy and dusty but ironically, as you pass the empty field where Camp Govey, one of Simpson Timber's old logging facilities, used to be, the road enters the National Forest and suddenly is paved. About four miles ahead, FS 23 enters the valley of the South Fork of the Skokomish. Drive all the way down to the bottom and cross the bridge. You are essentially there. The Brown Creek Campground is to the right. To get to the ride, turn left onto the 2353 road, cross LeBar Creek, and climb the hill past the two trailheads to the Skokomish River Trail. At the top of the rise, park where the 2353 splits in two.

Description

Linton Rowan cruising the Le Bar.

I have always enjoyed looking at the valley of the Skokomish's South Fork. It's big and wide and the sides curve gracefully upward towards the ridgetops. Even during the height of the clearcutting, the brown fields didn't diminish my appreciation for the immense and telling shape left behind by the glacier that carved it. A forest fire swept through the valley a few hundred years ago and the Douglas firs that grew up afterwards were in their prime when Simpson logged them. The few remaining stands, plus the corridor at the bottom of the valley, provide a hint of what the forest was like before we cut it down. I just hope we can wait and nurture the thick new fuzz of trees into their full potential before harvesting them. Then we need to nibble slowly and not let our greed decimate the forest again. Logging as slowly as the trees mature is the essence of sustainable forestry.

The ride to the top of LeBar Ridge and then back along the south flank of LeBar Creek provides a continuous look into the valley, trees and maturation process. It also provides a steep ascent, a couple of downhill blasts, and a long section of more technical single track—all elements of a good ride.

From your car, start off by riding up the leg of FS 2353 that branches off to the north from the main road. The grade climbs steadily and after about 1.75 miles comes to a switchback that is also an intersection with an abandoned road leading into the LeBar Creek drainage. That's the return route. Keep riding up the hill. A long mile later, the grade levels off and follows the top of the ridge for nearly two miles. Then it descends steeply towards a saddle. Before reaching the saddle, turn sharply to the right onto the uphill end of the abandoned road that started back at the switchback. It's hard to miss. There is an informal fire circle on the stub of old road at the intersection.

The Forest Service left a faint trail on the old roadbed when they decommissioned the double track, and following it may take an act of faith. If you decide not to, you can avoid busting back over the ridge by following the 2353 down to the saddle in the ridge. To get back to your car, turn left, or south, and descend to the bottom of the Skokomish Valley. That's not a bad road ride either, and if you want a strenuous diversion you can ride uphill from the saddle to the pass between the South Fork and Lake Cushman, described in the Dry Creek Ride (E5).

I prefer the dynamics of the trail down the LeBar Creek side valley. The Forest Service dug wide ditches, or swales, across the road at nearly regular intervals and these dips provide some technical thrills and challenges for the likes of me. Not too many people have used this path either, and it needs some TLC. A few volunteers with steel rakes, shovels and an axe or small chainsaw could easily clean up this trail so that a middle-aged dirt duffer like me could fly down the path without stopping.

Even the way it is, this portion of the ride is a worthwhile and enjoyable adventure. Scenically, it might be a little hard to take at first because the slopes of the valley were thoroughly logged and are still in the early stages of recovery. The new forest is just starting to cover the visible scars. This stretch of single track is nearly four miles long and once into it, you develop a feeling of being somewhere you don't want to get hurt because it's a long crawl back to the road. Thus, the ground is regaining qualities of wilderness. It's easy to imagine getting knocked out and waking up face to face with a curious black bear or cougar. After a short pull uphill, the trail reconnects to the 2353, which from there on provides a final speedy descent if you parked at the bottom. The more I think about this ride, the more I like it, and in my mind it is one of the best loop rides on the peninsula.

South Fork Skokomish River

Map 7

Synopsis: Classic single track through classic old growth timber

Distance: 5 miles one way

Elevation Gain: 300′

Time Required: 3 hours round trip

How to get there

Follow the directions to the South Fork of the Skokomish in Ride S1, LeBar Ridge Loop. Proceed all the way to the bridge just upstream from Brown Creek Campground, cross the river, and turn left onto FS 2353. About half a mile up the road, there are two trailheads for the South Fork Trail, one for hikers and one for people on horseback. I don't suggest using either if you have a bike but if you want to be official, use the horse trail to get started. The South Fork Trail starts off by going over a hump along the river and the horse trail begins a little higher. To get to the best place for launching this bike ride, drive past the two trailheads and turn onto the first spur road, #120, to the left. This turnoff is practically across the road from where I suggested parking for the LeBar Ridge Loop. Drive south into the trees towards the river and park where the road necks down to a trail. This single track converges with the main trail on top of the knoll and it's a lot flatter and smoother than the other two legs from the trailheads.

Description

The Skokomish Trail lies within a corridor of old growth that the Forest Service saved along the bottom of the valley, and the most difficult part of this ride is keeping your eyes on the trail while cruising past the huge trees. The trail enters the big timber almost immediately. Dropping off the top of the plateau provides a little bit of technical challenge in the beginning but once you're back down alongside the stream the trail is smooth and rolling for the next several miles. There are plenty of access points and campsites along the river and at times it is difficult if not impossible to see the old clearcuts on the sides of the ridges. A lot of extra gravel seems to have been deposited in the river, though, which is a result of quicker runoff times for

Big trees on the South Fork of the Skokomish.

rainwater down the logged-out valleys. As long as we, the caretakers of this land, never allow such an intense logging effort to occur again, the pulse of hydrology will slow down to its historic rhythm.

For the first three or four miles, the trail is fairly smooth and gentle but further on it becomes more challenging as the valley begins to narrow. The corridor of old growth leads to a large chunk of roadless area at the upper end of the valley that is unprotected by wilderness designation. The trail runs all the way through to the high country and National Park about 15 miles from the downstream trailhead. It's also feasible to leave the river bottom by Church Creek Shelter and travel over the ridges to the east into the Satsop, Wynoochee and Humptulips drainages. That's the direction this guidebook follows. If you're only out for a day trip, ride until the trail gets too technical and/or you tire out. My guess is that will occur in about five miles. Then turn back. The return trip will allow you to see the forest from another angle. Because the grade following the river also reverses, you will be able to carry a little more speed. Enjoy the cruise.

South Fork of the Skokomish

Satsop Lakes via Church Creek

Map 7

Synopsis: Sweaty ascent on road and technical up/down on trail over pass to lake

Distance: 4.5 miles one way

Elevation Gain: 2100′

Time Required: 4 hours round trip

How to get there

Again, follow the directions into the South Fork of the Skokomish given in Ride S1, LeBar Ridge Loop. This time, near the bottom of the hill just before the paved road crosses the river, turn left, or west, onto the graveled leg of FS 23. FS 23 runs along the south side of the old growth corridor in the bottom of the valley for 3.5 miles at which point it reaches a junction where it veers uphill to Spider Lake. Although there are some good camping spots up there, don't go that way. Stay to the right at the junction and follow FS 2361 another three miles to Church Creek and the Church Creek Shelter, which is down in the woods next to the river. Proceed another half mile up the 2361 and park at the junction with FS 2363.

Description

The Satsop Lakes sit in a corridor of old growth that extends from Olympic National Park along a ridge of mountains separating the upper Skokomish drainage from the Satsop and Wynoochee. These small lakes are west of the ridge and only a quarter mile from a road, the FS 2372, on that side. Church Creek is on the east side of the ridge and the trip I am about to describe is the hard way to the lakes.

From the 2361 down on the Skokomish, head up the 2363. This road ascends the southern base of Mt. Church alongside Church Creek. Three miles from the bottom, and 2100 feet higher in elevation, the road turns back to the north at an intersection with an abandoned road. Turn onto the abandoned road. It drops down a little ways and crosses the upper end of Church Creek to another short abandoned road. Most of the original forest is intact and I found myself wondering why they made such a great effort to build roads way up there, even though I was once vested in the logic behind cutting down every tree.

There are a lot of similarities between these bike rides and backcountry skiing. A person who understands why a skier or snowboarder will spend a few hours sweating uphill to slide down an untracked snowfield of powder in 20 minutes will appreciate taking a bike over the unnamed pass to Satsop Lakes. If you aren't into carrying and pushing your bike a little ways then leave it behind and walk up to the top of the ridge on the trail that starts on the other side of the road. Once out of sight of the road, this stand of ancient forest feels deep. It's only about a quarter of a mile to the top of the ridge and a mile from there to the lake. The trail is smooth and clean in most places. There are some rough spots that are too technical for me to coast through and a couple of others that I imagine anyone would have to carry their bike around. That said, it only takes 10 minutes or so to let gravity pull you from the pass down to the lake. Of course you then have to push and carry your bike back to the top of the ridge, which is a grind, but remember, from there it is a 2400-foot drop back to the car. Those who really enjoy downhill technical riding have the added treat of being able to descend the hiking trail on the south bank of Church Creek. That portion of single track isn't very long and it empties onto the 600 spur, the road that I suppose wiped out the lower end of the trail. From there on the grade is steep and fun to coast down. The 600 spur intersects the 2361 to the south of the bridge over Church Creek a half mile from where I recommend parking your car.

Over the course of 30 years I have walked the short way into the main Satsop Lake from the 2372 probably five or six times. There are 2 lakes and the trail goes to only the larger one. Although it was completely surrounded by big trees I never thought the pond was very attractive in the way you would expect it to be. There was something depressing about it, something missing. The massive logging outside the thick buffer zone had degraded the woods far beyond the dog hair (small trees) and new windfalls at the edge of the clearcut. When I decided the trail past the lake over to the Skokomish was the best route for the Circle Trail, I figured that other people would probably enjoy the run through the old growth and past the lake more than I would. Thus when I went back in the fall of 2006 and rode, pushed, and carried my bike from the lake to the pass, I was pleased to find the lake had changed. The water and trees were prettier than my recollection. No logging had taken place in the vicinity for over 20 years and the surge of new growth on the ground surrounding the island of virgin forest had restored the missing quality in the older trees. Or perhaps it was just a change in me.

The main Satsop Lake.

Wynoochee Lake Trail

Maps 7 & 8

Synopsis: Long, tough, physical test on single track around lake

Distance: 12 miles

Elevation Gain: 100′ over and over again

Time Required: 5 hours

How to get there

The upper Wynoochee valley is easy to find despite the long drive from the megalopolis on Puget Sound. The most expedient way to get there from Seattle is to drive down I-5 to Olympia and follow the signs to Aberdeen and Ocean Shores via the highway across the base of the Olympic Peninsula. This highway experiences three name changes. First it's U.S. Highway 101, then State Highway 8, and at Elma it turns into U.S. 12. Immediately past Montesano, get off U.S. 12 before it crosses the bridge over the Wynoochee River. Then head directly up the Wynoochee River Road for nearly 35 miles to Lake Wynoochee. The pavement ends about halfway there, and the drive will seem to last forever. Eventually you will see the first big trees at the edge of the National Forest looming above the second growth, which indicates that the drive is almost over. Grisdale, the last residential logging camp in the lower 48 states and my mailing address years ago, once stood just a mile beyond the boundary, but Simpson Timber Company closed the camp in

1985 and tore it down.

A mile past Grisdale take a left onto Forest Service Road 22 and then a few hundred yards later turn north onto the 2294. The dam and the Coho Campground are only a mile away. Park at the little lot at the trailhead below the east, or left, abutment of the dam (Left and right on a river are determined when looking downstream). You can also drive up the road a few hundred more yards to the recreational area where there are restrooms, picnic tables and a swimming beach. A sign warns people that the gate into the facility will close at dusk.

The ride clear around the lake takes a while and if you start any time past noon you might not make it back before nightfall. It terminates in the Coho Campground next to the recreation area so if you have a campsite there, good deal. Before 9/11, it was permissible to ride across the top of the dam but the authorities have put a stop to that. Therefore, the lakeshore trail dips down to the road and crosses the bridge above the plunge pool in front of the dam, which is no big deal.

Note: FS 22 runs southwest out to the Donkey Creek Road which then intersects Highway 101 north of Humptulips. That too is a good route in and out of the Wynoochee, especially if you are coming from the ocean or down from Quinault.

Description

The Army Corps of Engineers built Wynoochee Dam in 1972 to control floods and supply industrial water to Aberdeen. In 1992 Tacoma City Light tapped a pipe into the reservoir behind the structure, connected it to a new powerhouse, and began generating electricity. Unlike the dams due north on the Elwha River, the Wynoochee Dam has fish passage facilities that allow salmon and steelhead to get upstream so nobody has been clamoring to tear it down. When the reservoir is full the lake is also aesthetically pleasing. On calm days the surface mirrors the ridges along the sides and the squat yet regal mountain named Three Peaks at the far end. A tuft of old growth surrounds the shore, and during the rainy season, which is long and intense, loons call to one another across the water.

Starting out, heading up the east side, the trail climbs past the left abutment of the dam and begins following the edge of the plateau or bench above the high-water mark. As is typical on the flats surrounding the lake, the first stretch is in second growth and the single track is in good shape. You can make good time through these segments. Just over a mile from the dam, the trail dips down through the gully of the first side stream, which slows the trip down quite a bit. If you're technically adept, you'll probably enjoy maneuvering into these draws. But most people will have to carry and push their bikes up the short slopes on the other side. Regardless of ability, everyone is likely to enjoy the scenery in the ravines because most of them are filled with old growth and there are funky footbridges across the streams at the bottoms. This repetitive variation in the terrain pretty much defines the ride around the lake. Crossing through the ravines is tiring but every one has a unique stand of timber and presents something new to see.

On the east shore of the lake there are two spots where spur roads come in from FS 2270, the main line that runs up that side, so you can bail out and shag it back to the parking lot on the road or hitch a ride. One is about halfway up the lake and the other is near the end.

Towards the northern end there are also a couple of fairly long stretches where I had to push my bike. Again, someone with more dexterity and endurance may find those spots to be an enjoyable challenge. I was relieved to finally drop to the flats along the river above the mouth of the lake. That's a real scenic spot too. There are a lot of cool big trees, the river flows naturally, and the scars of human incursion are minimal.

At this spot you have to decide whether to continue up the left bank of the river to where the trail merges with the main road and crosses a bridge, or wade across the stream. If the river is low, I think you should wade across, if for no other reason than to feel the current on your legs. On the other side, follow the ribbon hanging from the vine maple on the gravel bar to the trail on the bank, and then take the leg headed upstream. I naively made the mistake of following the trail back down to the lake and soon got caught in a quagmire of blown-down trees. Not expecting the mess to stretch very far, I kept inching ahead but the trail only got worse. Most of the path was through old growth so the fallen trees blocking me were big and numerous. One barrier was three logs high. Lifting my bike over logs, dragging it underneath, and wading through the brush with it on my

The Wynoochee.

shoulder became a nightmare. Windfalls had covered a good mile of trail and it took over an hour to get through.

To go around this mess, head upstream when you cross the river rather than following it downstream to the lake. The trail will eventually come to the 2244. Get on the road and turn back towards the south, thus bypassing the bad segment of trail. You might be so tired by then you'll want to ride all the way back to the car on the road. That's okay. But if you are game for more single track, and plenty of good stuff is left, there is an easy and fun way back to the shoreline. About 3 miles from where you got on the 2244, turn off onto the 360 spur. There is no sign but the old double track is recognizable by the remnants of a white lumber fence that used to be part of a roadblock. There is also a fire circle at the entrance and just beyond that a deep ditch to block motorized vehicles. This road has been blocked off for a long time. It's mostly covered with grass, a few patches of alder trees and some brush here and there. A faint and rideable path weaves its way along the old roadbed for three-fourths of a mile down to the lakeshore trail, which is clearly marked. From there, the ride resumes alternating between flat enjoyable cruises and scenic dips through ravines. Coho Campground is two miles or so away.

S5 Three Peaks Loop

Map 7

Synopsis: Old logging road around a mountain, with a big climb and nice descent

Distance: 17 miles

Elevation Gain: 2600′

Time Required: 4 hours

How to get there

Follow the directions to Grisdale and Wynoochee Dam as described in Ride S4, Wynoochee Lake Trail. At the crossroads just beyond Grisdale, rather than turning towards the dam and Coho Campground, go straight and drive up the east side of the reservoir on Forest Service Road 2270. A mile or so past the end of the lake you'll come to a metal gate, which is open in summer. Immediately thereafter, the 2270 splits in two. Turn left towards a bridge across the Wynoochee River. Find a place to park on either side. There are plenty of spots to pull off plus some good campsites along the river.

Description

This trip follows the old logging road, the 2270, around Three Peaks, the mountain at the head of Lake Wynoochee. The first two logging shows I worked on at Grisdale were next to this double track so I have a sentimental attachment to the ground it crosses. When I first started up there, the cloud cover kept me from getting a good look at the surrounding country for at least a month even though it was summer. The sky wept continuously. Partly because we were yanking huge logs off a vast sloped field of downed timber as if they were toothpicks, I felt as far away from civilization as I could be. After a while, though, the bunkhouse and the West Branch of the Wynoochee began to feel like home. Survival there required a certain kind of toughness and disregard for the rest of the world. It still does.

This ride is a good test of endurance. Starting at the bridge, I prefer to proceed clockwise up the West Branch of the Wynoochee River. In the first five miles, the road bends to the north then slowly swings back to the west as it climbs steadily to a sharp switchback below the head of the valley. After a 180-degree turn the road gets steeper and traverses across a rock face. A little ways further it swings around an abutment into the valley of the North Fork West Branch. The stream is a thousand vertical feet below. The reprods, or fields of replanted trees, on the old clearcuts are tall and fuzzy now. A half mile from the bend into the side valley, a spur takes off to the left, or west, towards the top of the ridge. That's the way to the West Fork of the Humptulips. You can't ride a bike all the way through but the

Wynoochee Falls.

Forest Service has rebuilt an old trail that climbs over the ridge. It's steep so you would have to carry your bike. A more rideable trail could be installed on the abandoned road over the ridge to the Humptulips.

To continue on the ride around Three Peaks, stay on the 2270. The road climbs for nearly two more miles to a pass between the West Branch and Chikamin Creek, which is a tributary of the Wynoochee's main stem. Now on the north side of Three Peaks, there is a noticeable change in groundcover and climate. Perhaps because this side gets less sun, the atmosphere suddenly feels more alpine and the snow can linger on the road in here through June. There are a lot of Alaska cedars in the remaining blocks of old growth. Some ponds are scattered about. For a side trip, head back south on a spur road that cuts across the south face of the mountain. There used to be a trail from the end of that road to Klone Lakes on Three Peaks' eastern shoulder. I don't suggest trying to find Klone Lakes without the use of a good map and compass. I imagine that a handheld GPS unit would be helpful but I haven't invested in one. I prefer the older technology and my instincts.

Back on the main road, it's an eight-mile coast down 2600 feet to the bridge where the ride began. While winding down the north side of the mountain, the road passes a trailhead for a non-maintained path into Olympic National Park and eventually crosses a bridge over the main river. Then the double track follows the Wynoochee downstream past Wynoochee Falls, which is a "must see." It's not a huge fall, probably only 20 feet, but the site is idyllic. Plus the ride down the path that now inhabits the old access road is fun. There used to be a campground down there, too, but the Forest Service quit maintaining it after the logging stopped and funding got scarce. A couple of unofficial campsites are still useable, though. In fall look for salmon in the big pool at the bottom. Wynoochee Falls is just two miles from the lower bridge where this ride begins, so you can ride up from that direction or even drive. The Forest Service closes and locks the gate down by the bridge between October 1 and April 30 so to see the falls then you'll have to walk in or ride a bike, which is fine by me. I wish the gate were closed all year round.

S6 Humptulips Trail

Map 8

Synopsis: Great single track in old growth with multiple wet river crossings

Distance: 8 miles round trip

Elevation Gain: Zero

Time Required: 3 hours

How to get there

From Grays Harbor head north on Highway 101. Twenty-one miles from Hoquiam the highway crosses the Humptulips River and then passes the Humptulips Store. About 3 miles from there, turn off 101 onto Donkey Creek Road. If you are driving down from the north, this turnoff is about 15 miles south of Lake Quinault. I've always thought that Donkey Creek Road is one of the coolest paved roads on the peninsula. There is seldom anyone on it and you have to fight the temptation to drive like a bat out of hell. If you can't resist, at least slow down while going around the corners. The road has long straight stretches and the curves tend to sneak up on you. About six or seven miles from the intersection with 101, the road swings to an eastern heading. Shortly thereafter turn north onto FS 2204, which runs up the West Fork of the Humptulips. A few miles later, just before crossing a high bridge over a gorge, park at the trailhead to the West Fork Trail.

Back at the turnoff onto the 2204, Donkey Creek Road morphs into FS

22 and continues another 15 miles to Lake Wynoochee, which makes this ride a good option if you are staying at Coho Campground. The 22 road is paved but narrow and it's a pretty drive.

Description

The Forest Service didn't log the upper reaches of the East and West Forks of the Humptulips as intensely as it did everywhere else surrounding the National Park and a lot of virgin timber still remains in those valleys. That's a big reason why the trail along the West Fork is my favorite single track on the peninsula. With fewer clearcuts, large flows of stormwater haven't scoured the stream as is typical in other drainages. The forest scenery is better than on the Skokomish or Quilcene. The trail is rougher too, providing more of a challenge. Staying on your bike requires a little attitude.

Along the Humptulips River, West Fork.

Another quirk about this trail I enjoy, probably because I am a fly fisherman and enjoy wading in streams, is that it keeps crossing the river and there are no bridges. Traveling on the West Fork Trail requires you to get your feet and legs wet. It is therefore part water sport and to get the most out of it you should do it on a hot sunny day and take a towel. You'll find plenty of big secluded pools around the bends from the trail crossings that are perfect for skinny-dipping.

The West Fork Trail is about 16 miles long so it's doubtful that you'll be able to ride it all in one day. Of course that may sound like a challenge to a lot of you. But like I say, the trail is rough and overgrown in places, which slows bike travel to a speed not much faster than walking or running when combined with all the fording. Fortunately, five access points divide the long single track into four equal chunks. The first is the lower trailhead where I suggested parking. Working up the river, the other four are the 080 spur, Pete's Trail, the Campbell Tree Grove Campground, and the upper trailhead. Both the 080 spur and Pete's Trail come down to the river off FS 2204. The Campbell Tree Grove, also on 2204, is right on the trail and stream. And the upper trailhead is at the head of the valley where the trail crosses the road and begins its steep climb over the ridge to the West Branch of the Wynoochee (See Ride S5, the Three Peaks Loop Ride).

To be honest, I've only ridden the lower segment and the section between Campbell Tree Grove and Pete's Trail. On another trip I wanted to ride the upper segment down to the campground but the Forest Service hadn't yet reconditioned the trail. Since then I have heard that they completed the job. From what I've seen, though, I believe that the lower section is probably the cleanest part of the trail. I had a gas on it anyway. When I started riding upstream I was thinking about going all the way to Pete's Trail, but by the time I got to the connection to the 080, I realized I didn't have the energy. Rather than heading up to the main road, though, I turned around and went back down the trail, which was the right choice. I still haven't had enough of that trail and am looking forward to going back. I'll probably take my sleeping bag, some friends and family, and sleep out on a gravel bar. Car camping at Campbell Tree Grove is also an excellent way to spend a long weekend. Make sure you take a bike.

Quinault Ridge

Map 8

Synopsis: Fairly easy ridge ride on gated and abandoned road

Distance: 5 + miles to the end of the road

Elevation Gain: Not much

Required Time: 2 hours round trip

How to get there

About nine miles south of Lake Quinault on Highway 101, or 33 miles north of Hoquiam, turn west onto Forest Service Road 2258. Proceed six or seven miles northeast to the gate at the top of Quinault Ridge. Park there.

You can also drive to the top of the ridge from FS 2204, the main access road along the West Fork of the Humptulips (See Ride S6, Humptulips Trail, for more information on the 2204). Immediately north of the high bridge over the gorge, turn east off the 2204 onto FS 2220, which by the way runs all the way out to Highway 101. A mile past the intersection with the 2204, just after the 2220 swings around a hairpin corner, turn right (north) onto FS 2280. It's about a 4.5 mile drive to the top of the hill. Of course you can ride your bike to the crest of the ridge if you want but this road feels too heavily traveled for my taste.

Stovepipe Mountain from Quinault Ridge.

Description

To the east of Lake Quinault, the west flank of Quinault Ridge is one of the largest unprotected roadless areas in the Olympic National Forest. The scenic ground cover of old growth forest ends abruptly at the road on top of the ridge, though, out of sight from the tourists below. This road, the 100 spur, stretches over 5 miles to the edge of the Colonel Bob Wilderness Area and once provided access to the logging shows on the east side of the ridge above the Humptulips. The Forest Service put a gate on the road years ago and after the logging stopped abandoned this double track to the likes of us. The grade bobs along the 2400′ contour line and provides a comfortable platform for a ride.

Starting from the gate, the road weaves from one side of the crest to the other, giving up quick views of Lake Quinault and the Pacific Ocean in the distance to the west. After a couple of miles it sticks to the east side of the ridge all the way to the end. The Humptulips Valley in the foreground is deep and well-covered with virgin timber and maturing second growth. Across the chasm, the two forks of the river embrace Moonlight Dome and Stovepipe Mountain, features that draw and hold the eyes. For some reason the topography along the upper reaches of the Humptulips is different than everywhere else on the peninsula. Typically, long high ridges flank all the rivers radiating outward from the core. But here, between Quinault Ridge and the Wynoochee, the terrain is more pinched up and twisted, as if it was created with the tips of

God's fingers rather than with the sides of the Artist's hands.

The further north on Quinault Ridge the road goes, the more it intrudes on the rock structure. You can see how the construction crews had to blast it into the ridge with dynamite. Now, ironically, it provides an example of the land's recuperative power. Boulders and slides have fallen onto the road. Water and freezing temperatures have begun to loosen the compacted surface material of the grade and break down the larger stones into soil particles. Grasses, brush and trees have also started to grow and eventually the road will disappear. Left on their own, Northwest forests attempt to expand back outward after being cut away. That is always good to see and the borderline of wilderness is definitely fluctuating outwards from the top of Quinault Ridge. Most anybody can pedal out and see this interplay. It's not a difficult ride. The 100 spur is the first of several gated roads on the west side of the peninsula that extend out from the wilderness core like bent spokes.

Natural road removal on Quinault Ridge.

The West End

I don't believe that human beings have the wisdom to consciously alter the Earth's weather. Nor do I have much faith that we will stop screwing up the atmosphere by burning too much fossil fuel until the consequences start touching us where it hurts, both physically and monetarily. However, there will be some pleasant consequences of global warming and one of those may be occurring now over on the west side of the Olympic Peninsula. Thirty years ago when I worked in the rain forest it wasn't unusual to have only a couple weeks of continuous sunshine in the summer. Now it seems as if we can count on a few months of sustained good weather with only intermittent periods of rain. My guess is that the benefits of this phenomenon will be short-lived. Sunlight and heat have the potential to ruin the temperate rain forest in ways that can make over-harvesting the trees look trivial and quaint. Hopefully, scenarios involving massive wildfires, insect infestations, and human migration to more habitable climes will be slower to develop than our ability to reduce emissions of CO_2.

Will we be able to save ourselves from ourselves? The suspense is nearly unbearable. It's becoming obvious that it's going to take a while for the collective consciousness in the United States and other industrial countries to turn the momentum of this ship. As individuals it seems we can do little more than drive fuel-efficient vehicles and vote for politicians who aren't beholden to the oil industry. In the meantime, though, we should not be so self-effacing that we cannot enjoy some extra sunny days. I appreciate the increased opportunity to be able to view the glory of the Olympic rain forest without the rain from June to October. The last several times I have driven through Grays Harbor County, there has been no fog and even Aberdeen and Hoquiam seemed like they might be nice places to retire. Seriously and instinctively though, I hope that the woods over there slowly disappear back into the mist rather than go up in smoke.

No place on the west side of the peninsula is benefiting more from global warming than Lake Quinault. The rustic architecture of the cabins and resorts surrounding the shoreline was designed to keep people comfortable when they were stuck inside for months on end by the rain and darkness under the forest canopy. When the sun bursts out now in summer, it stays long enough for people to get in the habit of leaving their raingear behind when heading into the woods. Rain or shine, Lake Quinault has always been a beautiful place and like its sister bodies of water, Crescent and Cushman, has been attracting tourists for 100 years.

The only downside for me is that no trails connect Lake Quinault to the good bike rides I found on either side of it. Some day that might change. On the east side of the lake, a dirt road up Wright Canyon climbs about halfway up Quinault Ridge before ending. A Forest Service employee named Pete Erben has flagged a route for a single track from the dead end to the road on top of the ridge (See Ride S7, Quinault Ridge). Heading in the other direction, a new trail could be sited on an abandoned road northwest of the lake that follows a stream through the National Park into Forest Service land, and from there up to a road (the 2190) atop the ridge on the west side of Lake Quinault. From there, it's not too difficult to find a potential route all the way to Forks. Pete Erben has also blazed a trail for a segment of new single track from the end of the 2190 to the road on Matheny Ridge (the 2170), the location of the first ride on the west side I describe. Of course the Queets and Hoh Rivers block the continuity of a longer ride but I like to think that pedestrian suspension bridges can be built across these streams. Other than that, I found a lot of great shorter rides that can be done in the here and now, especially on my trips between the two big rivers.

Geographically, the Clearwater River, which flows into the Queets, drains the country between the Queets and Hoh. The eastern edge of the catchment marks the boundary of Olympic National Park. Nearly the entire basin is owned by the state and managed by the Department Of Natural Resources, or DNR. State law dictates that it be managed as a working forest to support public schools, so some logging is still going on. No more old growth is being taken out, not much of it is left, but the state is thinning the vast stand of maturing second growth. Some of the larger second growth at the lower elevations is even being totally liquidated now. The rate of the harvest will fluctuate with the political tide, I suppose, but I doubt if it will ever approach the volume reached when dozens of crews drove into this state forest each day, cut and yarded virgin timber as fast as they could, and trucked it to export yards in Port Angeles and Aberdeen for shipping to Japan.

In the meantime, the DNR will likely continue to maintain most of the roads built to haul the timber out. This infrastructure is something we all should take advantage of. Branching off the Clearwater-Hoh Mainline, a paved forest road that runs north and south through the area, roads lead east up every ridge and river bottom to the edge of the National Park. Each one of these double tracks is gated and the only members of the general public permitted through are those traveling under the power of their own muscles. Better yet, the views into the Olympic Mountains from these angles are awesome and seldom seen by anyone besides loggers, hunters, and foresters. The new trees on the old clearcuts close to the Park are still small and it is going to be decades before any logging resumes up there. That leaves plenty of time to hash over different land use strategies. I urge you to go up there and take a look.

The rides into the Clearwater all make excellent day trips when you are staying out on the ocean at Kalaloch or inland at Lake Quinault. The trips to the north, the ones up along the Hoh and particularly those north of the river, are more convenient to the Forks and La Push areas. There are lots of motels in Forks and campgrounds are all over the place. I particularly like the DNR campgrounds because they are more primitive and remote than the mainstream state parks and big federal compounds. The Upper Clearwater and Copper River Bottom are among what I consider the best places to car camp on the peninsula.

Whenever I go over to the west side of the peninsula, or the West End as the locals call it, I feel as if I am entering a vast playground. Mountain biking is just one of the activities in the mix of hiking, mountain climbing, river running, trail running, fishing, hunting, surfing and beachcombing—to name more than a few. It's all pretty woodsy over there, and often times wet, even in these early days of global warming. Trees and water, you'll get plenty of those.

Matheny Ridge

Map 9

Synopsis: On double track, a strenuous ascent then an easy ride beyond a gate

Distance: 8 miles from gate to end of the road, 15 miles from bottom of the hill

Elevation Gain: 2400' from bottom of road, 2800' from Queets River

Time Required: 4-5 hours from the bottom of the hill

How to get there

Driving west on Highway 101 from Lake Quinault, turn right, or north, onto Forest Service Road 21. This intersection is about 11.5 miles west of Amanda Park on Lake Quinault, and about 14 miles east of the bridge over the Queets River out by the ocean. Drive nearly eight miles north on road 21 to its intersection with road 2170. If you are not interested in climbing the hill on a bike, drive seven more miles to the gate and park.

Description

This road provides the best hill climb on the west side of the mountains. It's in a remote corner of the National Forest where not many people venture. The road is surfaced with crushed rock, whereas the roads on the DNR

Sunset over the Pacific from Matheny Ridge.

land to the north are covered with round gravel. More on that later. I have not seen the views either because the weather was foul both times I went up there.

Starting at the bottom of the hill, it is a long ride up to the gate. If you don't feel the need to punish yourself, drive to the top and start there. The road beyond the gate, which is about halfway out on the ridge, is a sweet ride even in the rain. How the road changes once you are past the road-block is striking. With the decrease in traffic, the vegetation has crept in from the sides and given this portion of the road a more natural feeling. There is plenty of old growth along the way, and the grade stays fairly true to the 3000′ elevation contour line. This would be a good ride for athletic kids and young teenagers. You could also pull a trailer with a small child on this road.

For a more difficult and adventurous way to do Matheny Ridge, start all the way down on the Queets River. The Queets bottom is part of Olympic National Park. A slide has recently cut the access road up the long skinny corridor but a service road comes in from the south, just below Matheny Ridge. The Park Service has recently converted the service road into the main road to the campground and trailhead rather than repair the river road. About three miles below the Queets Campground, the double track juts uphill past the boundary of the Park into state land. Heading away from the Park, keep to the left and don't take any of the turns to the right for about a half-mile. Just before entering an old gravel pit, an overgrown and impassable road takes off to the right. That's the way to go. There's a faint trail through the brush and you'll have to walk your bike a short distance but it's not very far to the 2180 road on the other side. Ride south a mile on the 2180, turn onto the 2170 and head up Matheny Ridge for the hill climb.

Matheny Ridge on a wet day.

Yahoo Lake–Kloochman Rock Loop

Map 10

Synopsis: A fantastic loop with a hard climb and smooth cruise on paved stretch

Distance: 13 miles

Elevation Gain: 1500′

Time Required: 3 hours without stopping at the lake or rock

How to get there

If coming from Lake Quinault, turn north off of Highway 101 about 21 miles west of Amanda Park onto the Clearwater Road. It's also known as the Hoh-Clearwater Mainline, or the Hoh Mainline or any other variation of those words depending where you are on it or who you are talking to. The Mainline basically runs north and south between the Hoh and Queets Rivers and is paved all the way through. If coming from Kalaloch on the ocean, turn off 101 five miles east of the bridge over the Queets River. After driving 12 or 13 miles north of 101, take a right on the C-3000. The DNR does a good job marking the roads and there should be a sign pointing to the Upper Clearwater Campground, which is real nice. Just past the campground, the C-3000 intersects the C-3100. Stay right and take the 3100. In a few miles you will come to the intersection with the C-3140. There is a gate on the 3140 and that is where I suggest parking if you and your party have only one car and you are planning to do the whole loop. If you have two cars, you might want to consider leaving one at the gate and driving two more miles up the hill to the gate near Yahoo Lake.

If coming down from Forks and the north part of the peninsula, turn off Highway 101 onto the Hoh-Clearwater Mainline a half mile south of the highway bridge over the Hoh. See Ride W4, Owl Ridge, for a more detailed description. Stay on the mainline for approximately 17 miles then turn east onto the C-3000 as described above.

Description

Yahoo Lake and Kloochman Rock, plus the gates that eliminate vehicle traffic, make this the best loop ride on the peninsula. These features overshadow the only negative aspect of riding a bike in the Clearwater State Forest: the round gravel with which the DNR surfaced the roads. The round gravel makes riding up steep hills more difficult because the rear tire loses traction sooner than it does on crushed rock. When coming down these grades the tires don't hold it either, forcing speed demons to slow down to keep from spilling. That's my complaint about the surfacing material and the reason I don't tout the hill climbs in the Clearwater as much as I do on the rest of the peninsula. Everything else beyond the gates in the Clearwater is a pleasant surprise, especially since it is best seen from the seat of a bike.

I suggest riding this loop counterclockwise. I think you should also consider spending a night along the way. Someone in reasonably good shape should have no trouble riding the loop in a day even with stops at Yahoo and Kloochman. However, if you are arriving late in the day after a five-hour drive from Seattle, camping at Yahoo Lake would make a lot of sense, depending on the weather. Yahoo Lake is less than a mile inside the upper gate. It's a hundred or so yards off the road and the trail leading to it is not much of an obstacle. Although a clearcut surrounds half the lake, there is still something special about the spot. Perhaps the lack of big trees on one side focuses attention on, and highlights the beauty of, the ancient timber on the other side. There are a couple of camping spots and waking up there in the morning would be a delight.

Kloochman Rock is three long miles further out on the ridge. That sounds easy but after leaving Yahoo the road takes a little dip then begins climbing a long steep grade to the northern flank of the Kloochman formation. This hill gains 1000 feet of elevation and ends at a crossroads with C-3185. To continue on with the loop, and to take the official way to the top of Kloochman Rock, head down the 3185. A quarter mile further, turn off onto another spur, C-3180, that leads back to the short summit trail. However, after having a conversation with two elk hunters I met near the intersection of the 3100 and the 3185, I got the feeling that there is a more convenient trail over to Kloochman that follows the ridge upward from the intersection. I haven't looked for it. To tell you the truth, I haven't been to the top of Kloochman yet because it was raining heavily both days I rode out there.

Kloochman Rock is right on the boundary of the Olympic National Park. According to the hunters, it looks out over the Queets River and up towards Mt. Olympus. The 360-degree view also includes the Pacific Ocean. The Forest Service used to have a fire lookout there and recently the Park Service rebuilt the wood platform on top. Ropes have been strung down for people to hold onto as they scramble up the last pitch of rock to the top. I don't think it would be difficult to find a good place to camp in the vicinity, either.

A stand of old growth flanks the 3185 much of the way as it descends to Solleks River. The top part of the hill is gentle but the grades down the switchbacks at the end are extremely steep. Be careful. At the bottom cross the bridge and take a left onto the 3140. The 3140 follows Solleks River down the valley to the gate, where hopefully you have a car waiting. Riding this stretch is the cream of the loop because the road is paved just below the bridge, making the last five or six miles a blast.

Solleks Ridge

Map 10

Synopsis: A ridge ride past a gate with some challenging dips

Distance: 7 miles out to the end

Elevation Gain: 1000′

Time Required: 3 hours round trip

How to get there

Drive to the Upper Clearwater Campground on C-3000 as described in Ride W2, Yahoo Lake–Kloochman Rock Loop. Keep following the C-3000 after it crosses the bridge. The 3000 crosses Solleks River and then begins climbing Solleks Ridge. A few miles further a gate blocks the road. That obviously is the start of the bike ride.

Description

Pedaling a bike atop any of these ridges beyond a gate on a nice day is a memorable experience. Each ridge leads to the edge of the National Park and provides its own unique angle of the Olympic Mountains, most particularly the many glaciated peaks of the Olympus massif. The ride along Solleks Ridge is a little longer than the others and well-suited for folks who want to push themselves. The double track both drops and climbs as it wiggles along the crest of the ridge and reaches 3200′ in elevation at a high point near the end. From there it is easy to see how a couple of short lengths of new trail could connect a route from Yahoo Lake and Kloochman Rock on the ridge to the south, to Owl Mountain on the next ridge to the north, and then down to the Hoh. All of this would be way beyond the gates along the Park boundary so therefore it would be remote and uncrowded. Another thing to look at from Solleks Ridge is the huge slide that sloughed off across the valley near Yahoo Lake. This is the biggest slide I have seen in the Olympics that occurred as a result of clearcutting the land. Hopefully, such extensive cutting and damage is a thing of the past.

Elk hunters on mountain bikes

Owl Ridge

Map 10

Synopsis: Another, much easier ridge ride on gated road

Distance: 5 miles to end

Elevation Gain: 500′

Time Required: 2 hours round trip

How to get there

About 12 miles south of Forks, or about 20 miles north of Kalaloch, turn east off of Highway 101 onto the Hoh-Clearwater Mainline. You'll see signs pointing to the Olympic and Clearwater Correction Centers, which are prison work camps. The Mainline runs nearly due east for about seven miles, then swings to the south. At the end of the curve turn off onto the H-1000, then not far from there turn again onto the H-1500. Stay on the H-1500. It climbs the ridge and eventually comes to the gate. You can also drive up the hill on the H-1600. It's a little shorter and takes off from the H-1000 a mile down the road from the start of the 1500.

Description

I'm taking the liberty of giving the name of Owl Ridge to the ridge north of the Clearwater River, as I don't really know if that's its real name or not. The stream to the north is named Owl Creek and this ridge merges with the one to the north at a peak called Owl Mountain.

The ride along the top of Owl Ridge on the 1500 is a shorter and easier version of the one on Solleks Ridge to the south. It therefore provides a better alternative for people who don't want to push themselves too hard to get in and see the views. The grade doesn't fluctuate as much and the scenery of the backside of Mt. Olympus is just as spectacular. Owl Mountain also sounds intriguing but it has been logged on all sides and I passed it by. By then I was looking at a higher spike on the ridge further up the road on the edge of the National Park and sea of old growth timber beyond, covering the ridges like waves crashing onto the rocks of Olympus.

The climb to the top of the spike is a good workout. From the junction to Owl Mountain, the H-1500 dips down slightly then climbs a long steep grade. The road terminates at a saddle on the ridge, surrounded by old growth. A spur road to the left leads the rest of the way to the summit. Windfalls on the road force you to walk. Bulldozers scraped off a circular landing at the top but the sides of the knob never got logged and big trees completely ring the clearing, except for the road coming in. It's a good place to sit and meditate.

A decommissioned road to the Clearwater River in need of a trail.

There are two other routes into this area. One is to ride up Huelsdonk Ridge, which is gated. The other is to make the hill climb up to Owl Mountain and ridge from the South Fork of the Hoh on the 1080. That road is gated near the bottom, too. Using these other roads, you could do a loop ride while staying at the South Fork Campground, one of the more humble camping venues on the Hoh. Seeing Mt. Olympus is definitely worth the ride.

Peak 6

Map 11

Synopsis: A strangely enjoyable hill climb due to Scotch broom on road and fantastic views

Distance: 4 miles to top

Elevation Gain: 2800′

Time Required: 2 hours up

How to get there

Coming down from Forks on Highway 101, turn east onto the Upper Hoh Valley Road. This is the main road to the Hoh Rain Forest Visitor Center so there is plenty of signage. Pass the little campgrounds, the stores, and the old homesteads. When you are less than a mile away from Olympic National Park, pull off and park at the entrance of DNR road H-3900. The ride starts at the gate just a couple hundred feet from the main road.

Description

The ride up to Peak 6 is the best hill climb in the vicinity. However, it has a major quirk. Scotch broom covers the road a mile or so from the bottom. It's so thick in some places that pedaling uphill becomes impossible and you have to get off and push your bike. This barrier of invasive weeds lasts for about a mile until it finally thins out and disappears. The road

Crucifixion snag on Peak 6.

has another unique feature. About halfway up the hill, in the fringe of big old trees on the upper side of the road, you'll see a snag that looks like a cross with Jesus hanging on it. I kid you not.

About two-thirds or three-quarters of the way up, the 3910 splits off from the 3900. I don't think a sign marks the two different paths. But after the 3900 has completed its second major switchback and climbs to the east again, keep bearing to the right. My map shows three major 180-degree (almost) bends and this would be the second one when going uphill. Not far beyond this intersection, the DNR has pulled the culverts and decommissioned the road. It's pretty smooth, though, and the views of the Hoh Valley and of Mt. Olympus start getting good. The road goes all the way to a landing on the top of Peak 6.

Peak 6 is on the Bogachiel-Hoh Divide directly across the Hoh from the homestead built by John Huelsdonk and his wife, Dora. Huelsdonk was the legendary Iron Man of the Hoh. He got that name when another homesteader named Chris Morgenroth—the same Morgenroth mentioned earlier in the book who became a forest ranger and then spearheaded the effort to create the Olympic National Park—saw Huelsdonk one day on a trail south of Forks carrying a 110-pound cast iron stove on his back. Morgenroth asked his neighbor if the stove was heavy. Huelsdonk replied that it was, but it was the 50-pound sack of sugar in the oven that was giving him trouble because it kept shifting around. Hiring himself out as a pack animal was one way he earned money. He also supported his clan by bounty hunting for cougars. That was what made him famous. I couldn't help but wonder if he had seen the crucifix on the side of the hill, too, while following his pack of dogs.

The ride back down through the Scotch broom was surprisingly fun. I lost my bicycle pump, though, when I took a fall while crossing a little bridge. The next time I go up there I'm taking a machete.

Mt. Olympus and Mt. Tom.

Bogachiel–Hoh Divide

Map 11

Synopsis: Good hill climb for a DNR road, leisurely ridge ride, no gate, big views

Distance: 10 miles from the valley bottom, 5 miles from the top of the ridge

Elevation Gain: 2400′

Time Required: 3 hours one way from bottom

How to get there

This ride has an easy and a difficult version. If you want a good hill climb—the difficult version—follow the directions to the Upper Hoh Valley Road as given in Ride W5, Peak 6, and park at or near the intersection with the H-3100. The intersection is only a mile upriver from the cluster of buildings and businesses in the heart of the picturesque community along the upper valley. There is no identification sign at the intersection but the road branching off looks like a main road, there is a stop sign on it and the intersection is across from a guardrail along the top of a steep bank.

If you are only in the mood for a pleasant ride with fantastic scenery and want to skip the hill climb, I suggest turning off Highway 101 onto DNR road H-3200 three-quarters of a mile north of the intersection with the Upper Hoh Valley Road, or approximately 11 miles south of Forks. Stay on the 3200. It dips across Alder Creek then begins climbing the end of the Bogachiel-Hoh Divide. After the initial steep rise, the angle of the grade

The western Olympic skyline as seen from the Bogachiel-Hoh Divide.

line diminishes. Of course you can park and start anywhere you want since there is no gate on this road, but for the easy version of this ride I suggest going all the way to the intersection with H-3160. It was marked the last time I was there.

Description

The difficult version of this ride is not as technically challenging as the road up Peak 6 and is perfect for some sustained, aerobic exercise into the heights above the river. The grade up the initial leg off the Upper Hoh Valley Road is steep but indicative of the climb ahead. At the top of the initial hill, turn left at the intersection then ride a little less than 1.5 miles to the intersection with the H-3160. Again, there is no road marker but it is the only good road heading up hill off the 3100. Plus there is an old landing across the 3100 at the bottom, which makes an excellent place to park if you want to start this ride in a more remote setting.

Except for a short flat section about two-thirds of the way up, the climb is steep all the way up, so stand on your pedals and take the elevator to the top, 1600 feet in elevation from the bottom. Right. I sure wasn't able to. In fact I ended up walking my bike most of the way up. I like to think it was because I was using my bike with double suspension, and pedaling it while standing was more like jumping up and down on a pogo stick, but this climb simply kicked my middle-aged butt. I still think it's a great ride though. Like all other DNR roads, this one is covered with round gravel rather than crushed rock. However, for some reason it is packed tight in most places and real firm. Therefore, while descending you will be able to concentrate

more on speed management than on keeping your tires firmly on the road, though there are a couple of spots where that won't be the case. Either way, make sure your brakes are in good shape before doing this ride.

Another reason I like this climb is that currently, about halfway up the hill, a landslide has made it impossible for people to drive all the way through. Then there is the view at the top.

At the crest of the ridge, if you have any energy left, turn right onto H-3200. As mentioned earlier, this is a good spot to park if you drove up from Highway 101 and are doing the easy version of the ride. The road gains another 600 feet in elevation from the intersection to the dead end, five miles away, and the views make the air seem thinner than it is. Since the ridge serves as a boundary line for Olympic National Park, a vast blanket of old growth covers the Bogachiel drainage to the north. The Pacific Ocean is to the west, obviously, and south there is an eagle's view of the old homesteads at the bottom of the Hoh Valley. The mosaic of clearcuts on the hills beyond the river in that direction is the only negative I suppose, but now that they are green again discussing the different philosophies of forest management may be easier than it was a decade or two ago.

However, the main reason to go up there is to see the Olympic Mountains, not to have an argument. The slant from the Bogachiel-Hoh Divide offers the most complete glimpse of the Olympics' western skyline: from Mt. Carrie to the north, past the long spread of Olympus and all its ancillary peaks, to the Valhallas in the south. Perhaps the state doesn't gate off this road because everyone who loves the Olympic Peninsula should be able to travel to the top of the Divide. It's not Hurricane Ridge or Deer Park but the smell of salt is in the air and the sound of the homesteaders clearing their land in the rain forest still echoes up from below.

Forks Connector

Map 11

Synopsis: An anomaly for this book because it starts in a town

Distance: 7.5 miles from Forks to end of road on Elk Ridge

Elevation Gain: 1300′

Time Required: 2 hours one way

How to get there

It's real simple. Drive to Forks and park at Tillicum Park, which is on the north end of town next to Highway 101.

Description

To end this book I am going to describe a ride that is different than any of the previous ones. It doesn't go to a big view or into a patch of ancient trees. Instead, it leads back to the concept that inspired me to write this book: the continuous Circle Trail around the edge of the Olympic National Park. When I explored the larger route I found that the trail came closer to Forks than to any other town on the peninsula. Thus, because part of me will always be a logger and Forks once proclaimed itself to be the logging capital of the world, I started to think of Forks as the beginning and end of the trail.

When I presented my idea to some folks at the Forest Service, they told me that the local ATV crowd had actually worn a short trail between the end of a DNR road that led out of town and the end of a Forest Service spur road that connected onto FS 2932. That was cool. The Forest Service had abandoned most of the 2932, which led over Elk Ridge between the Bogachiel and Calawah Rivers, and I had already explored the old double track's southern segment up off the Bogachiel. As I looked at a map, it was easy to guess where this freelanced connecting trail was and when the time came, it was just as easy to find. Building connecting trails is an important part of the concept and to see them growing naturally, without planning and official sanction, was heartening. As I implied in the introduction, there is something basically human about finding and following travel corridors across the undeveloped landscape. Many of us need that connection not only to the dirt and the trees but to ourselves and one another.

This ride begins at the center of the town on Main Street. Turn east at the light onto Calawah Way, then follow it out of town for 2.25 miles and turn right onto Elk Ridge Road. Up to this point you have been doing a typical road ride through the countryside but now it changes. Within a quarter of a mile from Calawah Way, the road turns to dirt, starts climbing steeply, and passes through a gate. On the other side of the gate, the road (the F-5000), becomes a typical DNR logging road complete with round gravel. It also gets really steep as it mounts the end of Elk Ridge. Just about everybody will have to push their bike up that grade.

Elk Ridge isn't as high as the other ridges featured earlier. It's also covered with maturing second growth, which blocks the views. There are some new clearcuts along the F-5000 where you can see down into the Calawah but those end at the end of the road just under two miles from the gate. That's where the connecting trail begins. I guess it could be called a single track but it's wide enough for quads. The connector is only a hundred yards long or so and slopes downhill to the 030 spur off FS 2932. The connector and spur probably offer the best mountain biking on this route. It's about 1.25 miles over to the 2932 and once there you have the option of turning right and following Elk Ridge to the end of the road, turning left and dropping down to the Calawah River, or going back to Forks.

At the minimum, I suggest riding south for almost two miles to the end of the road. The grade climbs a little more and the new forest has enclosed the road. If you want more of a challenge, carry your bike around the roadblock and try riding on the old roadbed. The abandoned grade goes on for several miles and is very doable in places. At least walk out that way a little and see the recovering forest. It's doing a fine job of reclaiming the old road. This route over to the Bogachiel does need a trail, though.

Back at the intersection with the spur to the Forks Connector, you may also want to ride the 2932 downhill to the bridge over the Calawah, another short two miles away. The Calawah is wide and slow-moving in the vicinity of the bridge, very peaceful looking. On the north side of the bridge, the 2932 intersects FS 29 and if you turn right there you can follow the 29 all the way to the Sol Duc drainage and the first ride in this book. It's about 20 miles away. If you turn left you can ride 5.5 miles out to 101 and then another 1.5 miles down to Forks and your car, thus completing a big loop. The Klahanie Campground is just a half-mile from the bridge, though, and it's a nice place to pitch a tent. The Forest Service opens Klahanie only in the summer and it feels a lot further from town than it actually is.

Headed towards Forks.

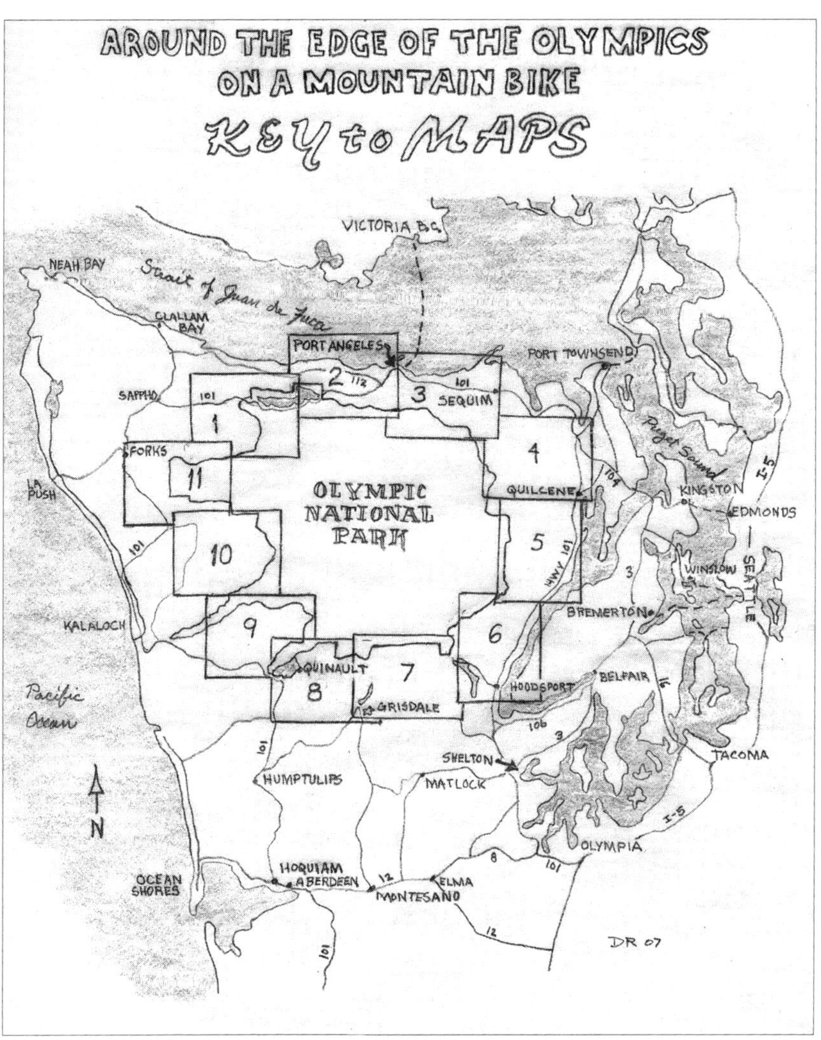
AROUND THE EDGE OF THE OLYMPICS
ON A MOUNTAIN BIKE
KEY to MAPS
VICTORIA B.C.
NEAH BAY
Strait of Juan de Fuca
CLALLAM BAY
PORT ANGELES
PORT TOWNSEND
SAPPHO
SEQUIM
FORKS
LA PUSH
OLYMPIC NATIONAL PARK
QUILCENE
Puget Sound
KINGSTON
EDMONDS
WINSLOW
SEATTLE
BREMERTON
KALALOCH
QUINAULT
GRISDALE
HOODSPORT
BELFAIR
Pacific Ocean
SHELTON
TACOMA
HUMPTULIPS
MATLOCK
OLYMPIA
HOQUIAM
ABERDEEN
ELMA
MONTESANO
OCEAN SHORES
N
DR 07

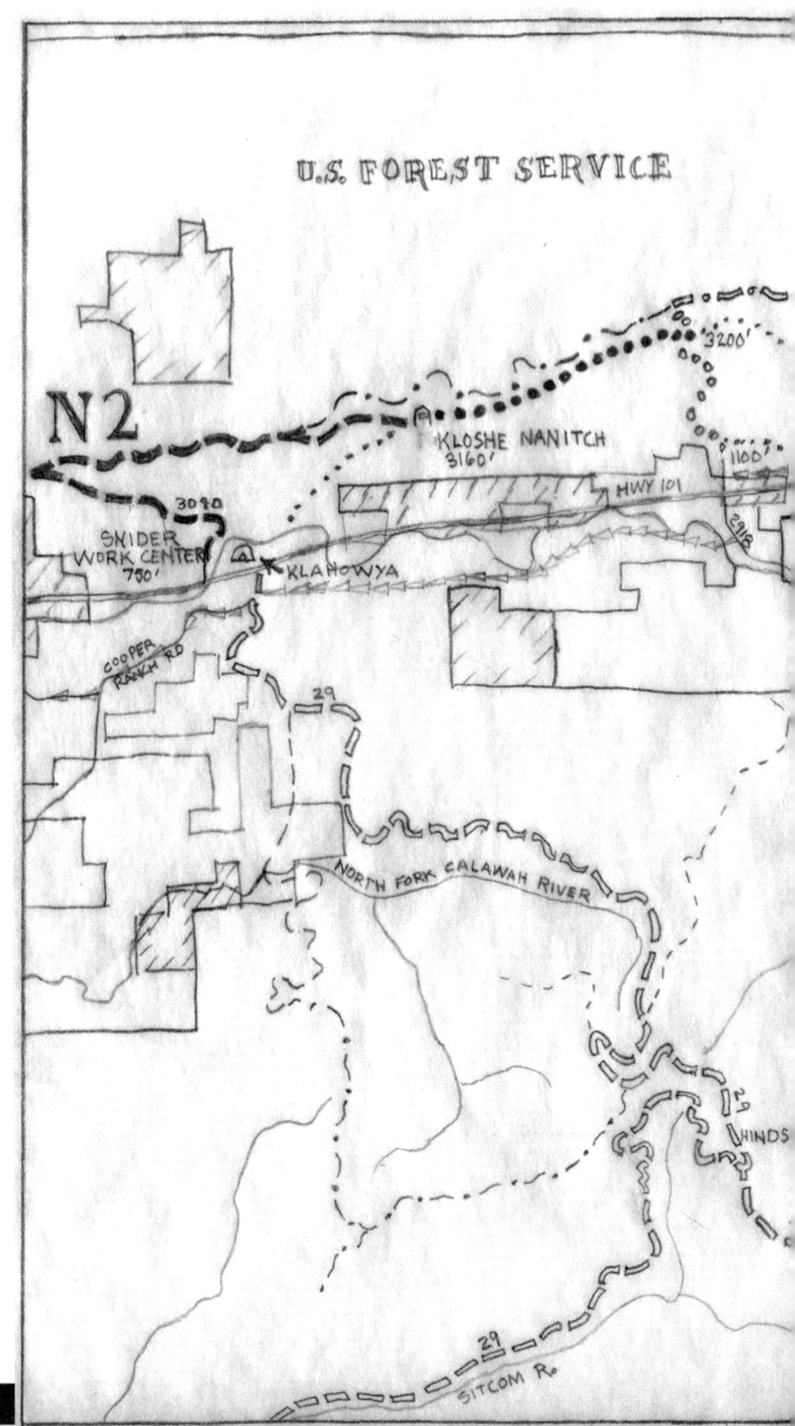
U.S. FOREST SERVICE
N2
KLOSHE NANITCH
3160'
3200'
1100'
HWY 101
3040
SNIDER
WORK CENTER
750'
KLAHOWYA
COOPER
RANCH RD
29
NORTH FORK CALAWAH RIVER
29
HINDS
29
SITCOM R.

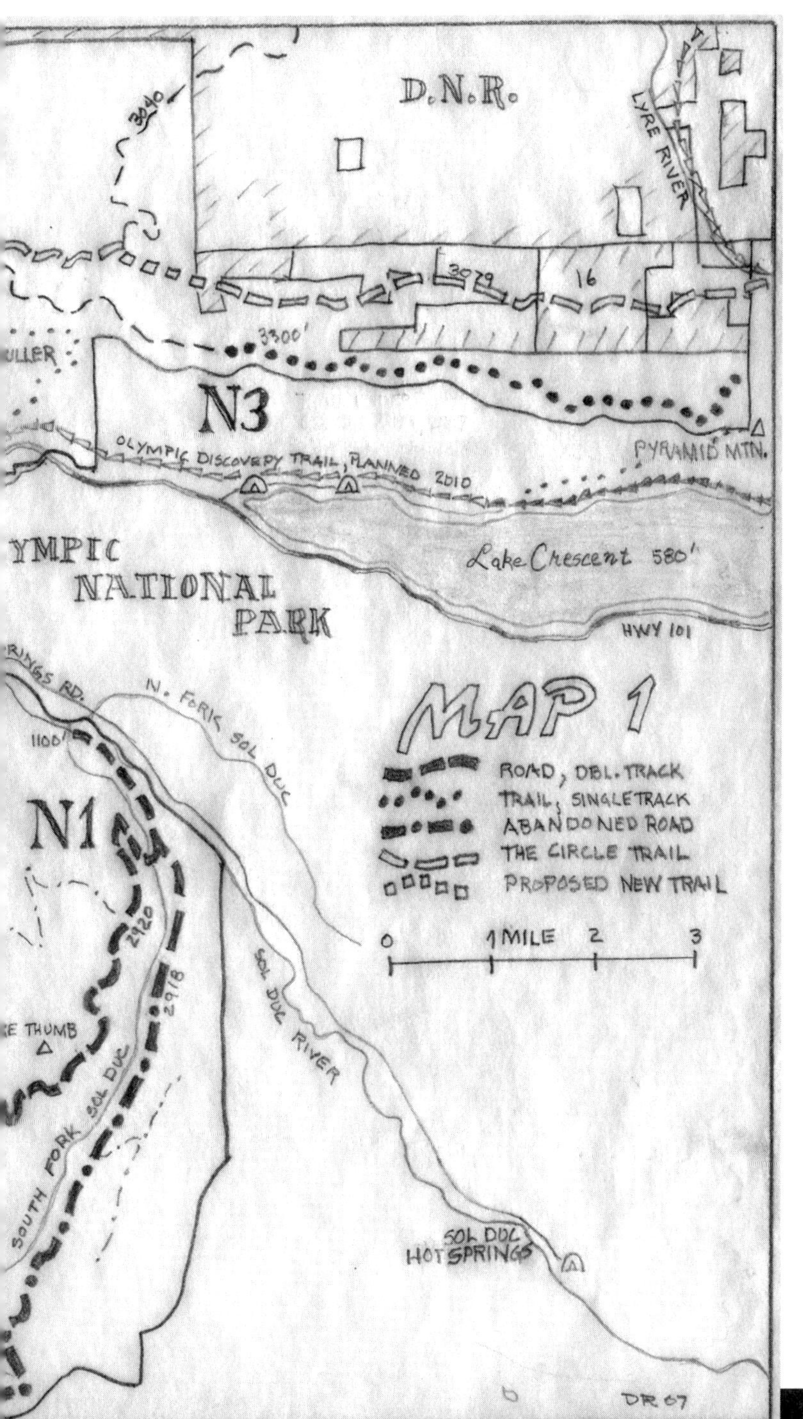

D.N.R.
3040
LYRE RIVER
3079
16
3300'
N3
PYRAMID MTN.
OLYMPIC DISCOVERY TRAIL, PLANNED 2010
Lake Crescent 580'
YMPIC
NATIONAL
PARK
HWY 101
RINGS RD.
N. FORK SOL DUC
1100'
MAP 1
ROAD, DBL. TRACK
TRAIL, SINGLETRACK
ABANDONED ROAD
THE CIRCLE TRAIL
PROPOSED NEW TRAIL
0
1 MILE
2
3
N1
2920
2918
SOL DUC RIVER
E THUMB
SOUTH FORK SOL DUC
SOL DUC
HOT SPRINGS
DR 07

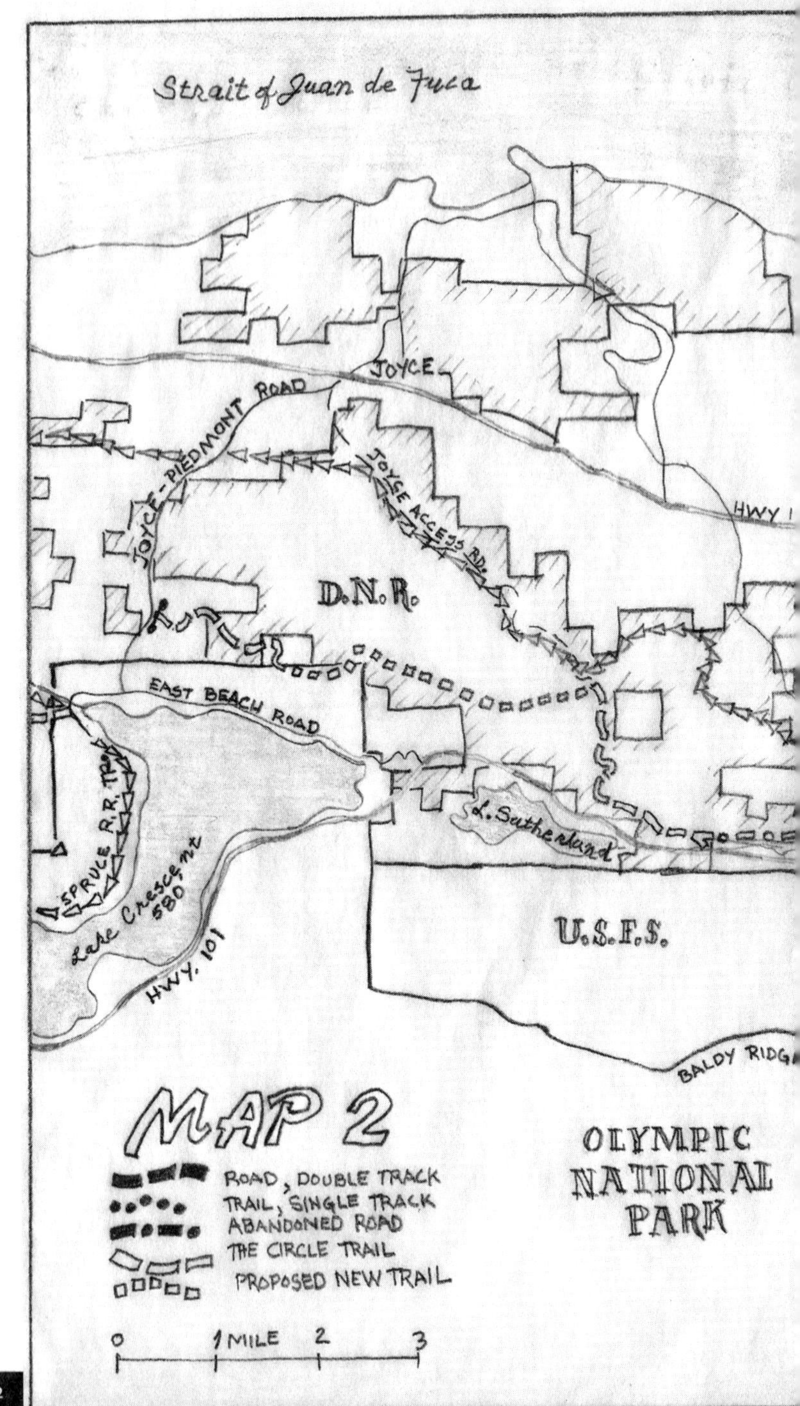

Strait of Juan de Fuca
JOYCE
JOYCE-PIEDMONT ROAD
JOYCE ACCESS RD.
HWY
D.N.R.
EAST BEACH ROAD
SPRUCE R.R. TR.
Lake Crescent
580'
HWY. 101
L. Sutherland
U.S.F.S.
BALDY RIDG
MAP 2
ROAD, DOUBLE TRACK
TRAIL, SINGLE TRACK
ABANDONED ROAD
THE CIRCLE TRAIL
PROPOSED NEW TRAIL
0
1 MILE
2
3
OLYMPIC NATIONAL PARK

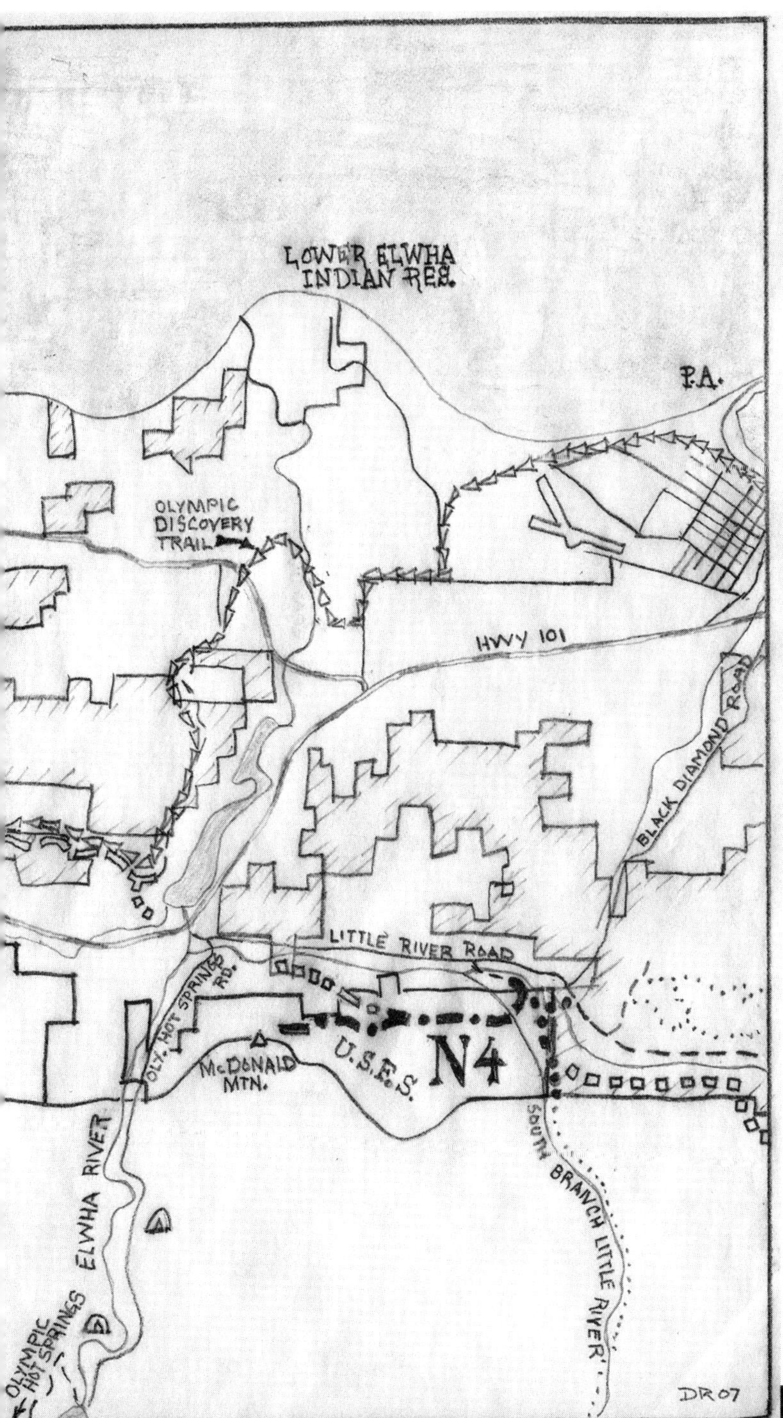
LOWER ELWHA
INDIAN RES.
P.A.
OLYMPIC
DISCOVERY
TRAIL
HWY 101
BLACK DIAMOND ROAD
LITTLE RIVER ROAD
OLY. HOT SPRINGS RD.
McDONALD
MTN.
U.S.F.S.
N4
SOUTH BRANCH LITTLE RIVER
ELWHA RIVER
OLYMPIC
HOT SPRINGS
DR 07

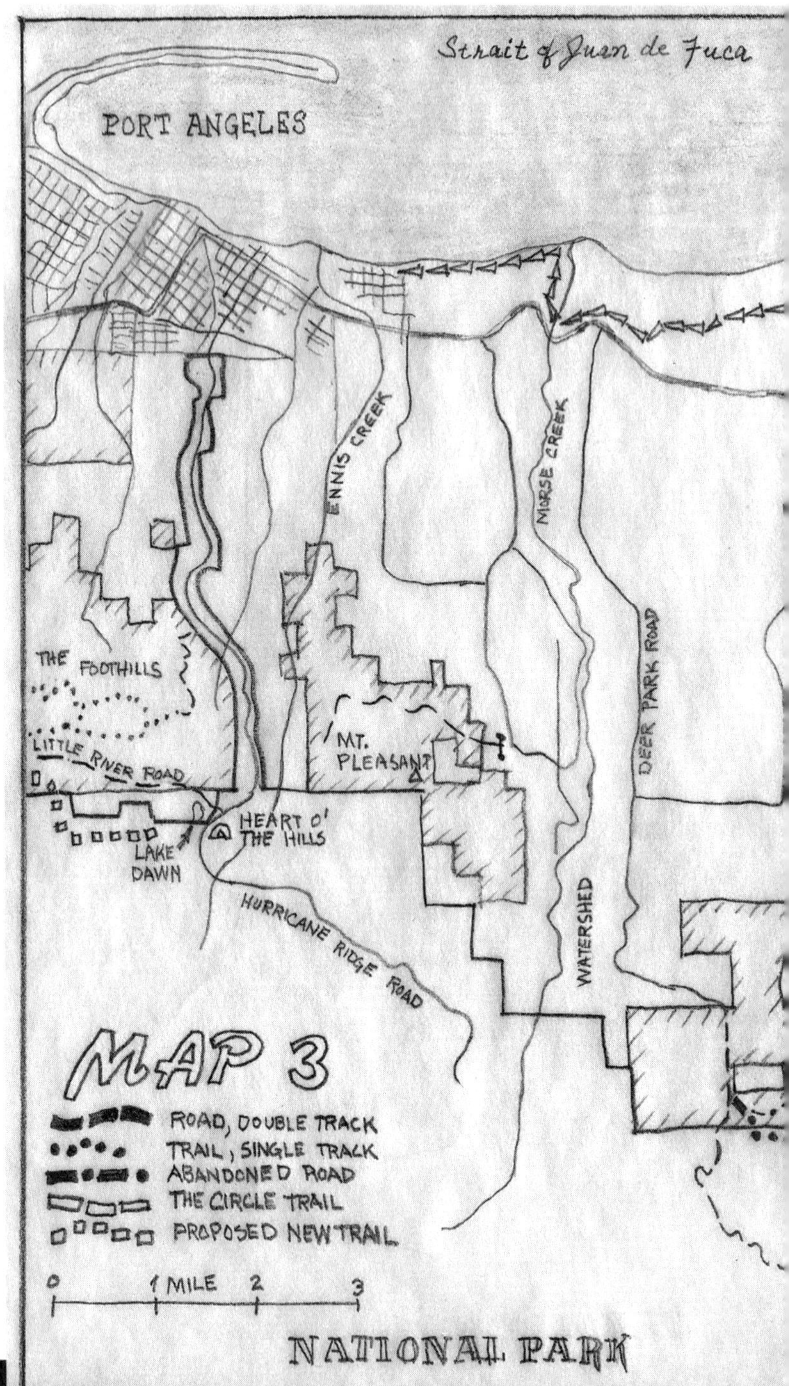
Strait of Juan de Fuca
PORT ANGELES
ENNIS CREEK
MORSE CREEK
DEER PARK ROAD
THE FOOTHILLS
LITTLE RIVER ROAD
MT. PLEASANT
HEART O' THE HILLS
LAKE DAWN
HURRICANE RIDGE ROAD
WATERSHED
MAP 3
ROAD, DOUBLE TRACK
TRAIL, SINGLE TRACK
ABANDONED ROAD
THE CIRCLE TRAIL
PROPOSED NEW TRAIL
0
1 MILE
2
3
NATIONAL PARK

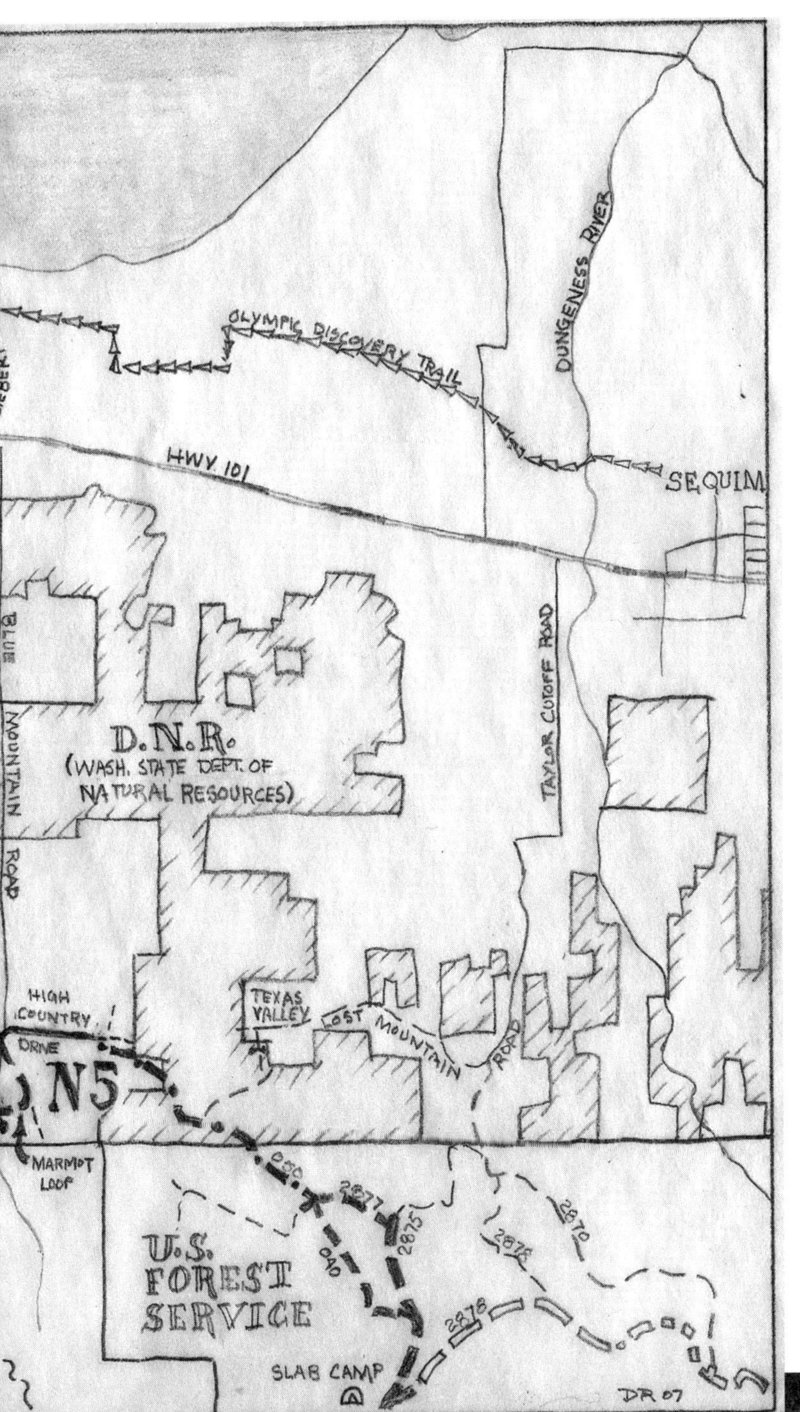

OLYMPIC DISCOVERY TRAIL
DUNGENESS RIVER
HWY 101
SEQUIM
BLUE MOUNTAIN ROAD
TAYLOR CUTOFF ROAD
D.N.R.
(WASH. STATE DEPT. OF NATURAL RESOURCES)
HIGH COUNTRY DRIVE
N5
TEXAS VALLEY
LOST MOUNTAIN ROAD
MARMOT LOOP
U.S. FOREST SERVICE
2877
2875
2870
2876
2878
SLAB CAMP
DR 07

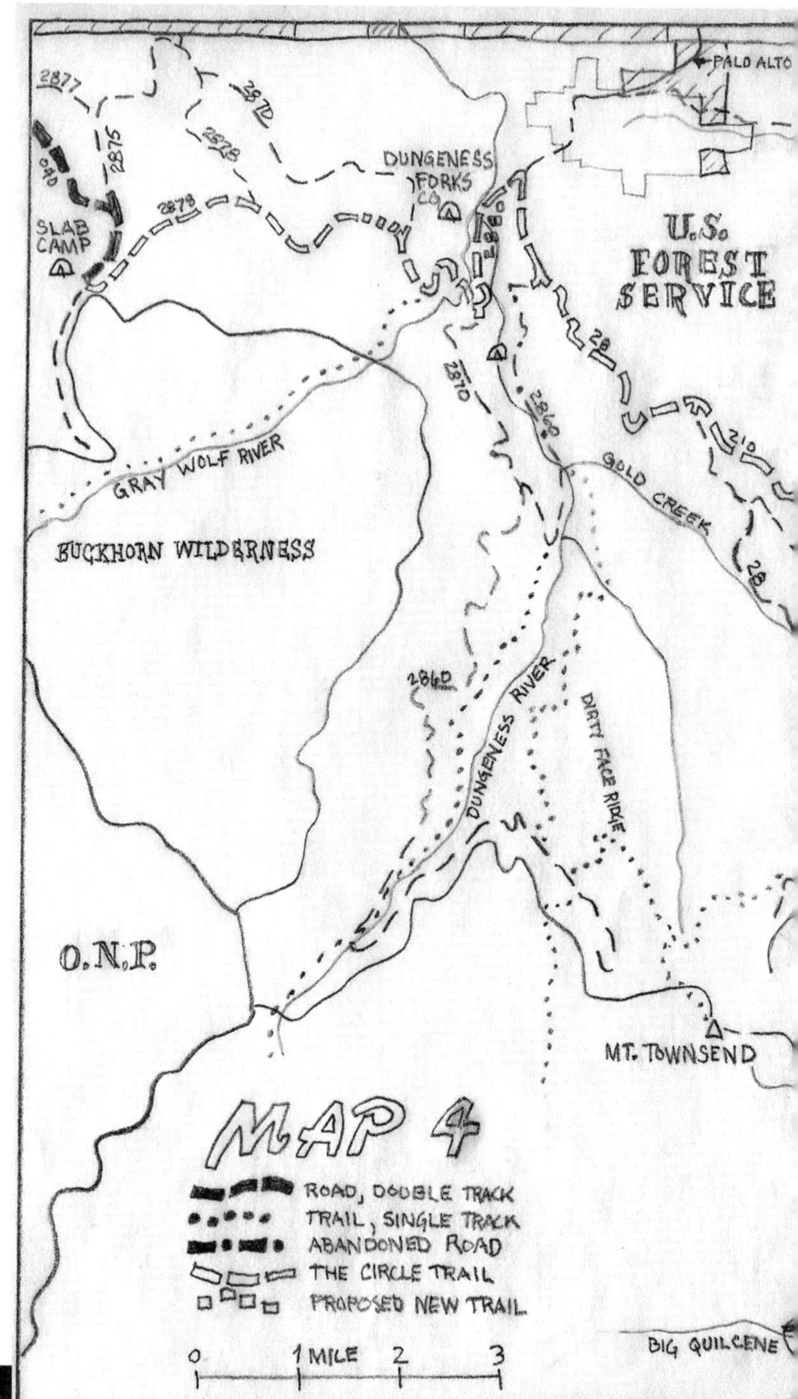

PALO ALTO
2877
2871
2875
2878
DUNGENESS
FORKS
C.G.
2878
SLAB
CAMP
U.S.
FOREST
SERVICE
28
2870
2860
210
GRAY WOLF RIVER
GOLD CREEK
28
BUCKHORN WILDERNESS
2860
DUNGENESS RIVER
DIRTY FACE RIDGE
O.N.P.
MT. TOWNSEND
MAP 4
ROAD, DOUBLE TRACK
TRAIL, SINGLE TRACK
ABANDONED ROAD
THE CIRCLE TRAIL
PROPOSED NEW TRAIL
0
1 MILE
2
3
BIG QUILCENE

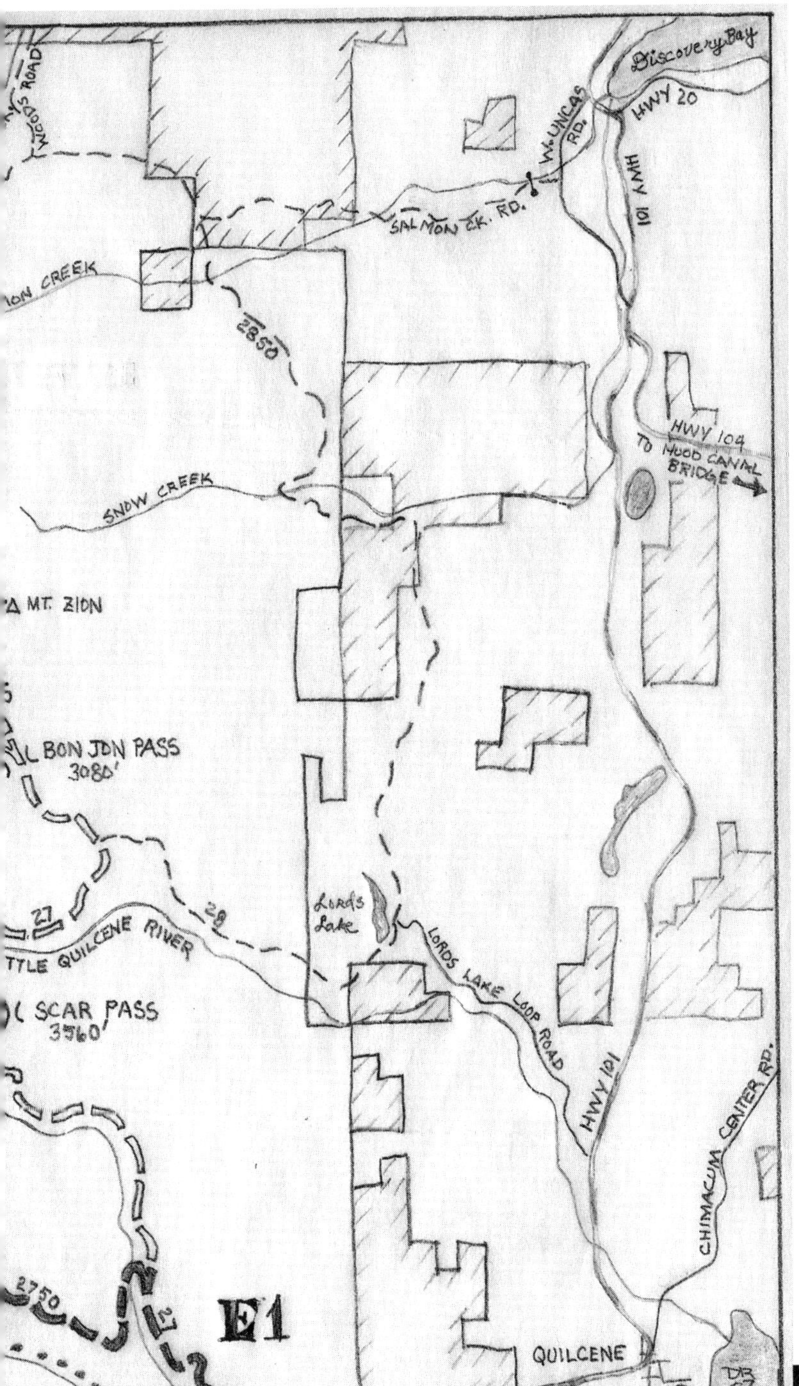
WOODS ROAD
Discovery Bay
HWY 20
W. UNCAS RD.
HWY 101
SALMON CK. RD.
ION CREEK
2850
HWY 104
TO HOOD CANAL BRIDGE
SNOW CREEK
MT. ZION
BON JON PASS
3080'
27
28
LITTLE QUILCENE RIVER
Lords Lake
LORDS LAKE LOOP ROAD
SCAR PASS
3560'
HWY 101
CHIMACUM CENTER RD.
2750
27
E1
QUILCENE
DR 07

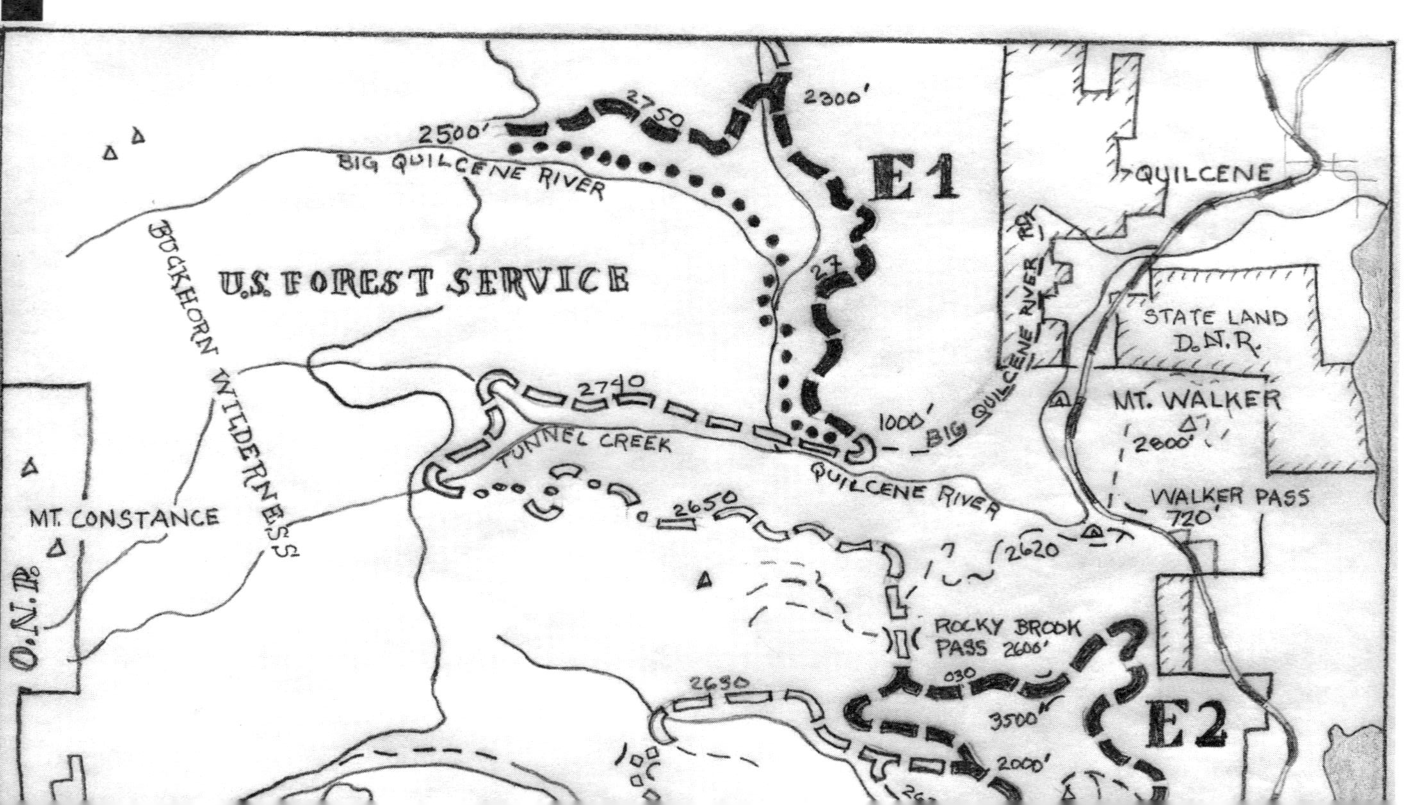

QUILCENE
STATE LAND
D.N.R.
MT. WALKER
2800'
WALKER PASS
720'
QUILCENE RIVER RD
E1
2300'
2750
2500'
BIG QUILCENE RIVER
27
1000'
BIG QUILCENE RIVER
2620
ROCKY BROOK
PASS 2600'
030
3500'
2000'
E2
U.S. FOREST SERVICE
2740
TUNNEL CREEK
2650
2680
BUCKHORN WILDERNESS
MT. CONSTANCE
O.N.P.

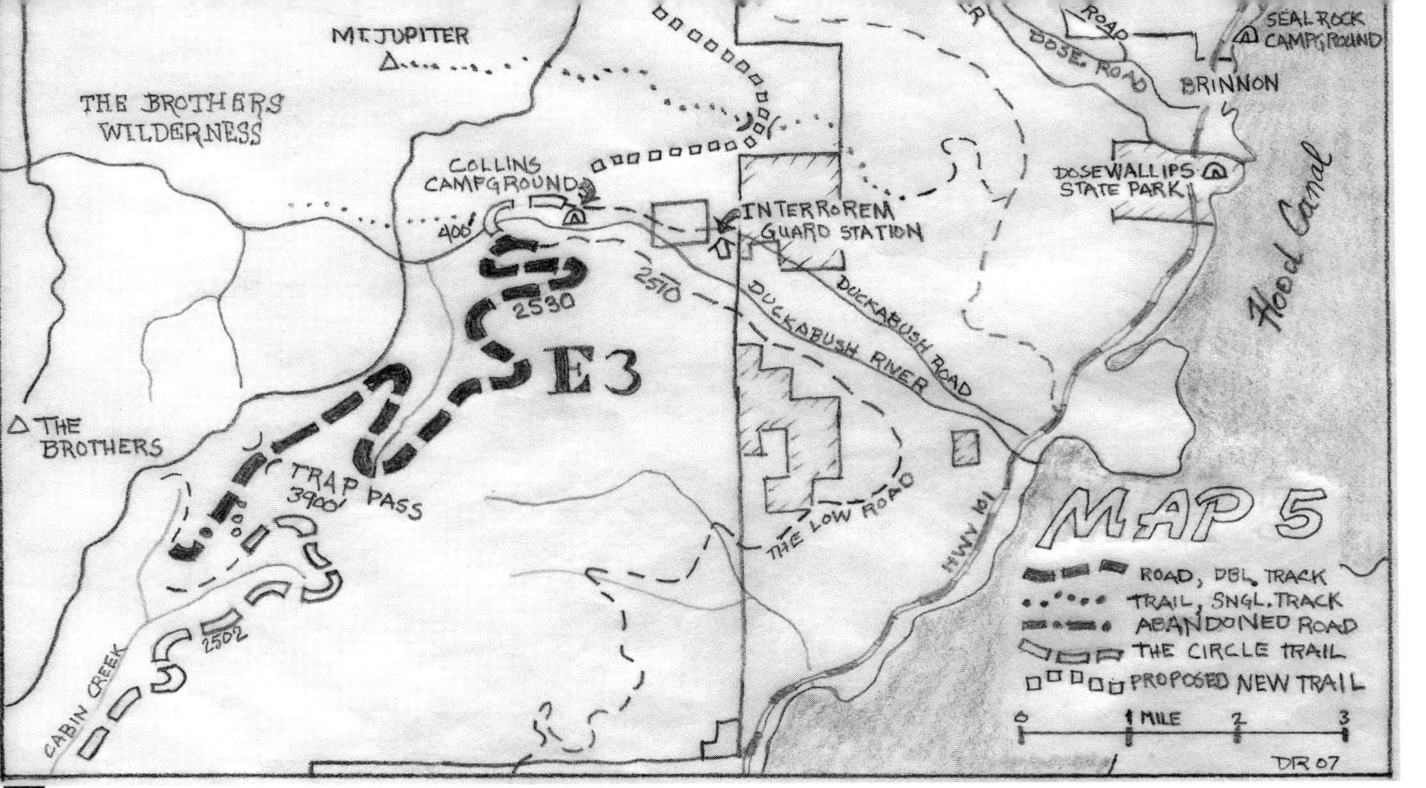
MT. JUPITER
THE BROTHERS WILDERNESS
COLLINS CAMPGROUND
400'
INTERRoREM GUARD STATION
2510
2530
E3
DUCKABUSH ROAD
DUCKABUSH RIVER
THE BROTHERS
TRAP PASS
3900'
2502
CABIN CREEK
THE LOW ROAD
HWY 101
ROAD
DOSE. ROAD
BRINNON
SEAL ROCK CAMPGROUND
DOSEWALLIPS STATE PARK
Hood Canal
MAP 5
ROAD, DBL. TRACK
TRAIL, SNGL. TRACK
ABANDONED ROAD
THE CIRCLE TRAIL
PROPOSED NEW TRAIL
0
1 MILE
2
3
DR 07

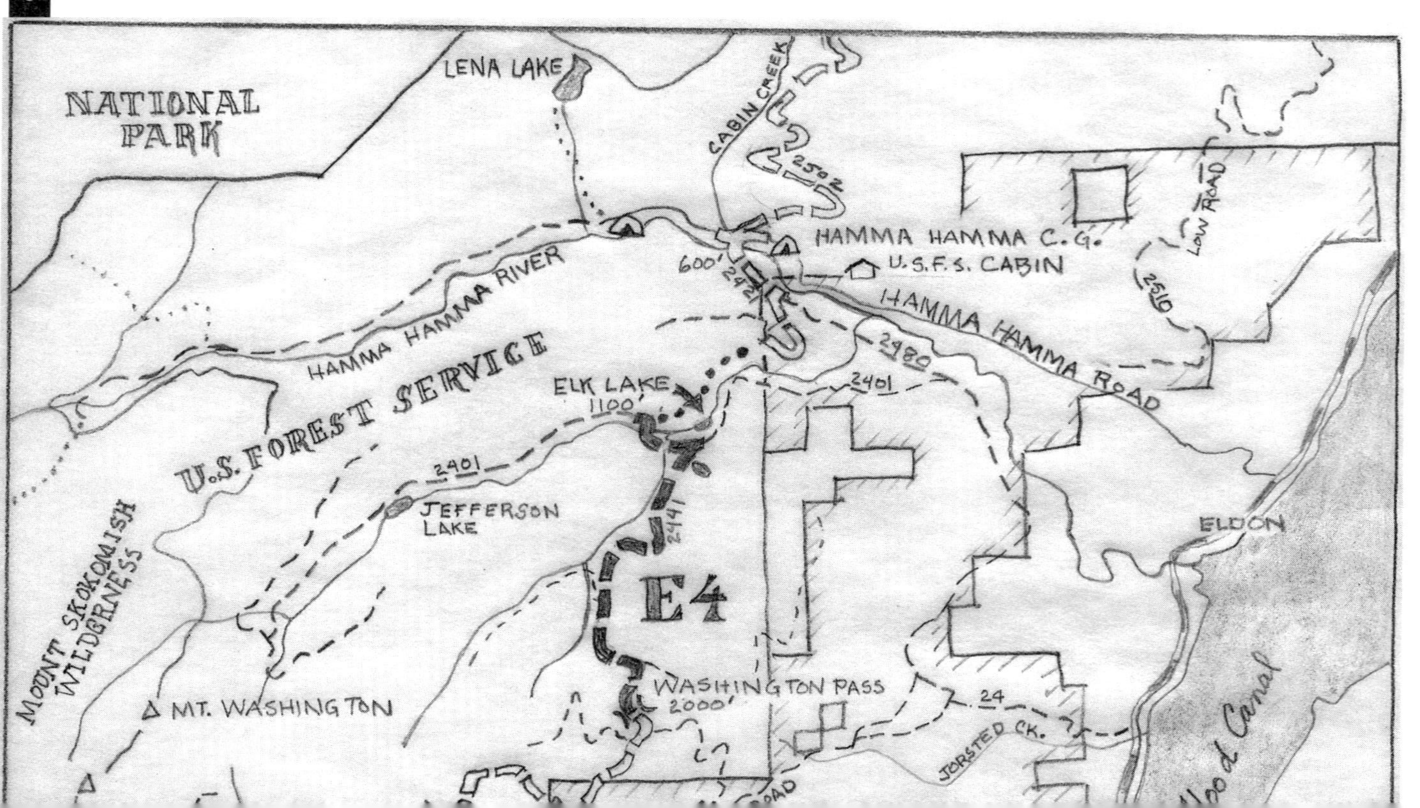
NATIONAL PARK
LENA LAKE
CABIN CREEK
2502
HAMMA HAMMA C. G.
U.S.F.S. CABIN
LOW ROAD
2510
600'
2421
HAMMA HAMMA RIVER
HAMMA HAMMA ROAD
2480
2401
U.S. FOREST SERVICE
ELK LAKE
1100'
2401
JEFFERSON LAKE
2441
E4
ELDON
MOUNT SKOKOMISH WILDERNESS
MT. WASHINGTON
WASHINGTON PASS
2000'
24
JORSTED CK.
Canal

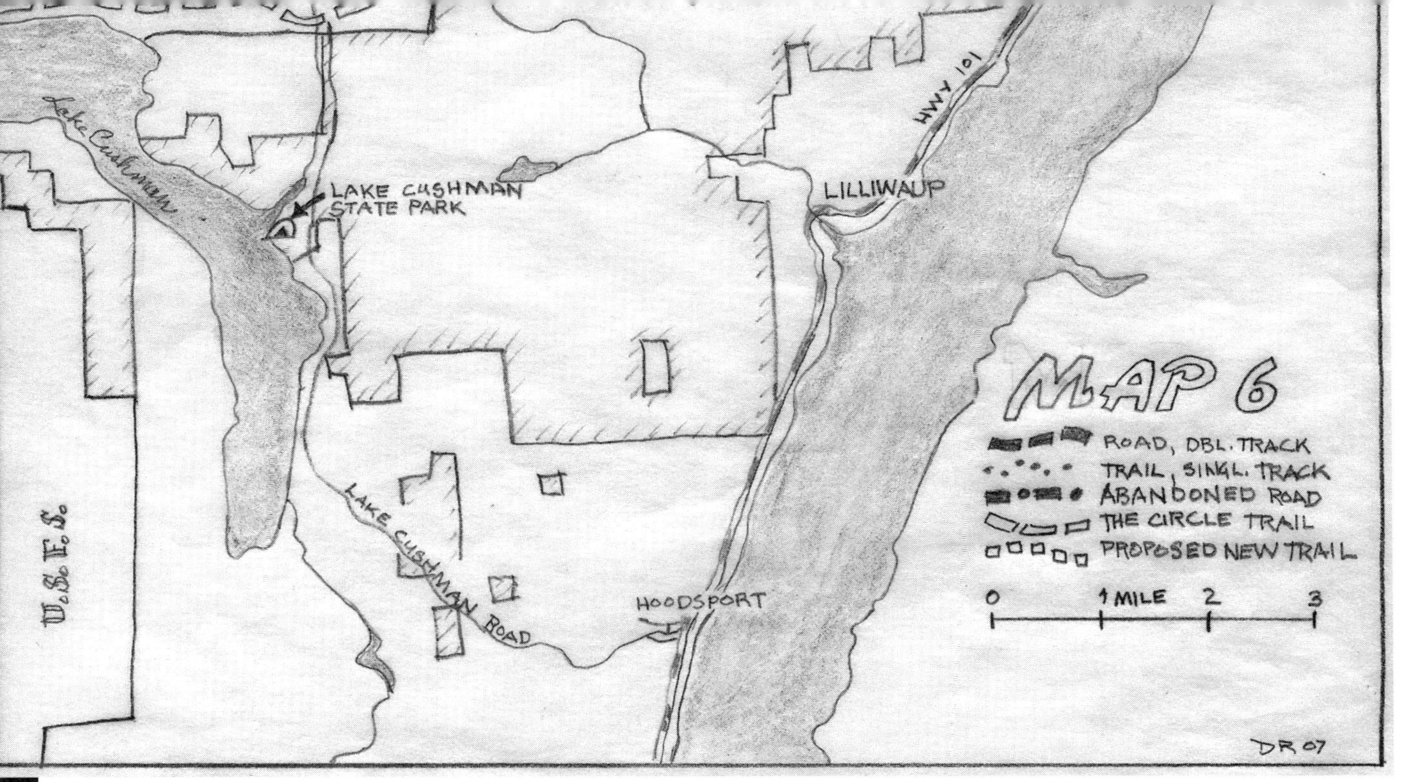

MAP 6
ROAD, DBL. TRACK
TRAIL, SINGL. TRACK
ABANDONED ROAD
THE CIRCLE TRAIL
PROPOSED NEW TRAIL
0
1 MILE
2
3
DR 07
HWY 101
LILLIWAUP
HOODSPORT
LAKE CUSHMAN STATE PARK
LAKE CUSHMAN ROAD
Lake Cushman
U.S.F.S.

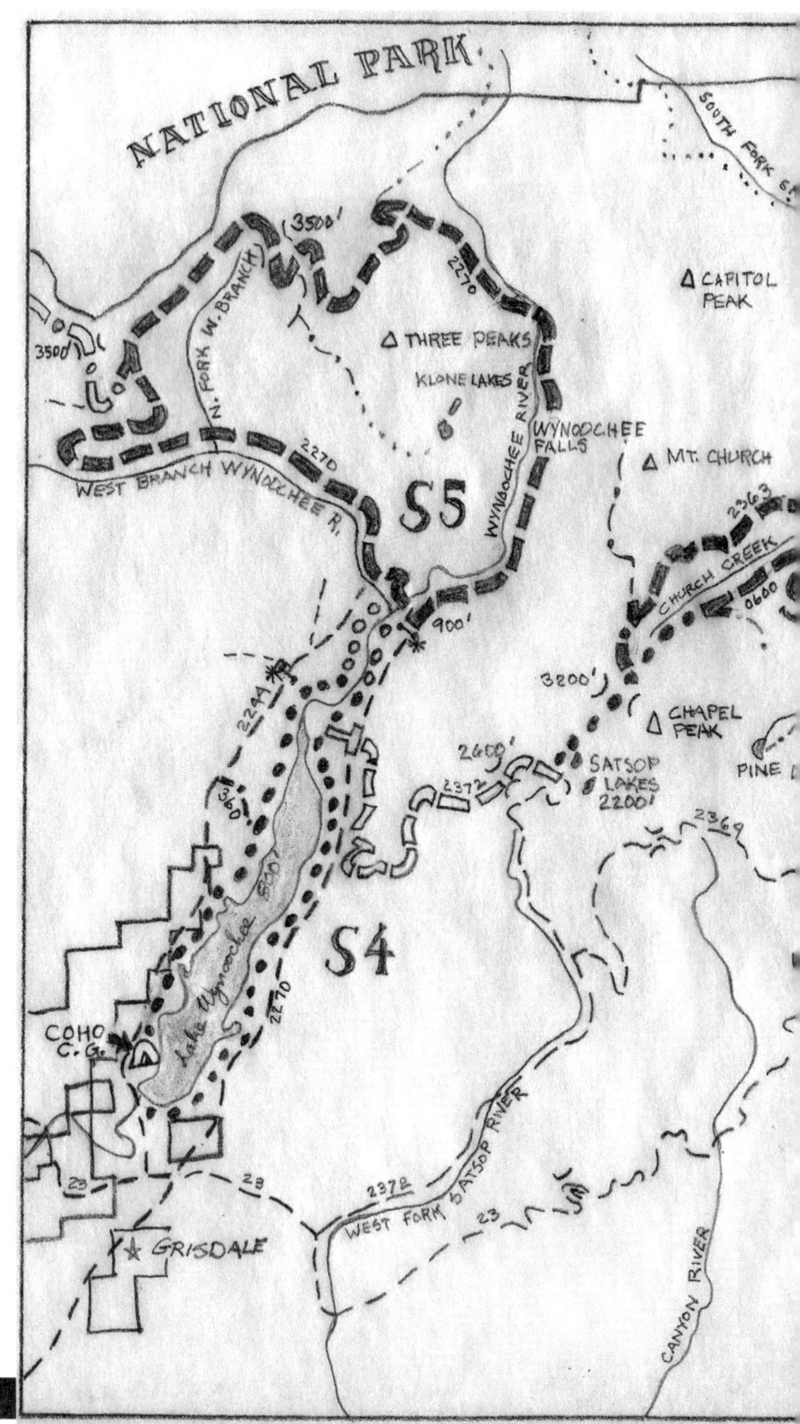
NATIONAL PARK
SOUTH FORK
CAPITOL PEAK
THREE PEAKS
KLONE LAKES
N. FORK W. BRANCH
WYNOOCHEE RIVER
WYNOOCHEE FALLS
MT. CHURCH
WEST BRANCH WYNOOCHEE R.
S5
CHURCH CREEK
CHAPEL PEAK
SATSOP LAKES 2200'
PINE
S4
Lake Wynoochee
COHO C.G.
GRISDALE
WEST FORK SATSOP RIVER
CANYON RIVER
3500'
2270
900'
2363
0600
3200'
2600'
2372
2369
2294
060
2270
23
2372
23

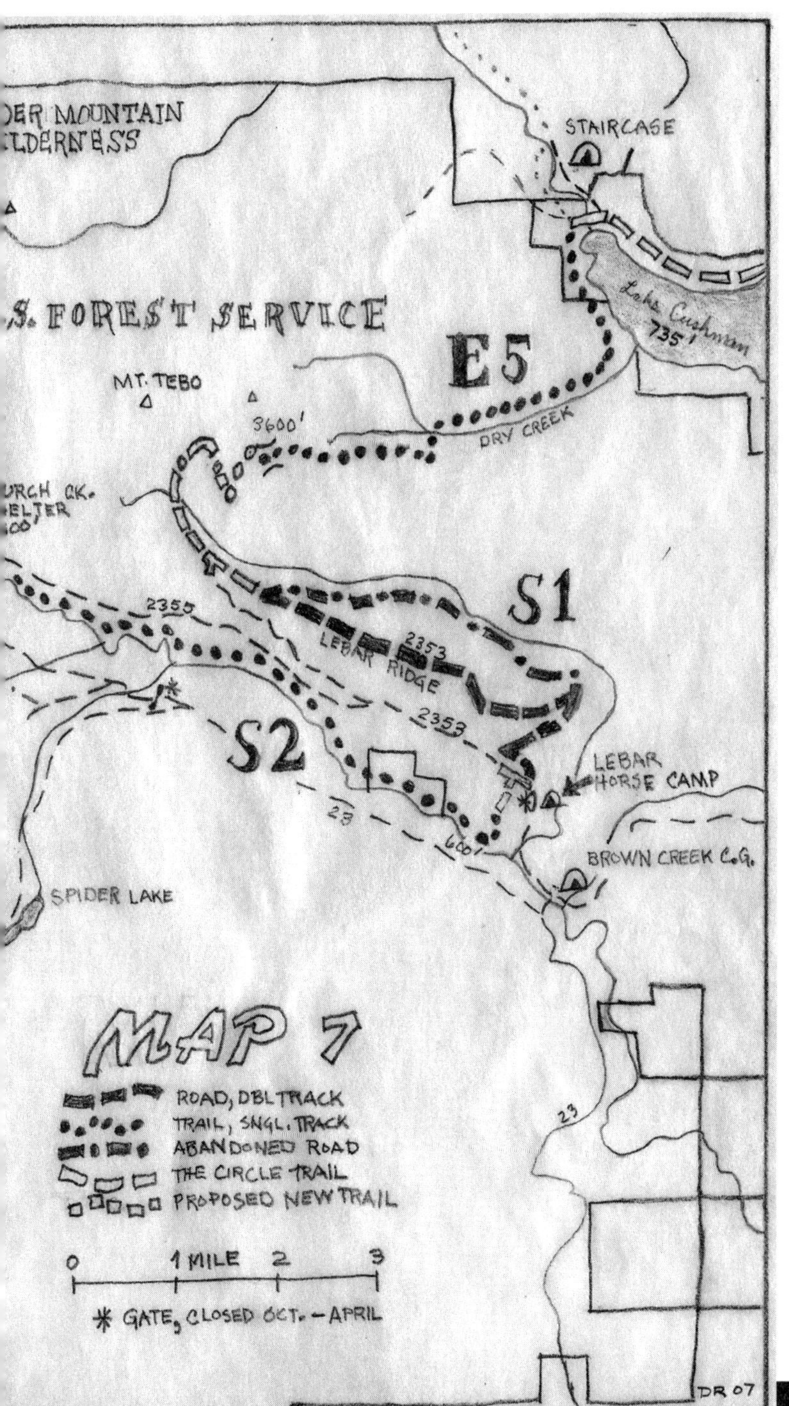

STAIRCASE
Lake Cushman
735'
E5
MT. TEBO
3600'
DRY CREEK
S1
2355
LEBAR RIDGE
2353
2353
S2
LEBAR HORSE CAMP
23
600'
BROWN CREEK C.G.
SPIDER LAKE
MAP 7
ROAD, DBL TRACK
TRAIL, SNGL. TRACK
ABANDONED ROAD
THE CIRCLE TRAIL
PROPOSED NEW TRAIL
0
1 MILE
2
3
* GATE, CLOSED OCT. – APRIL
23
DR 07

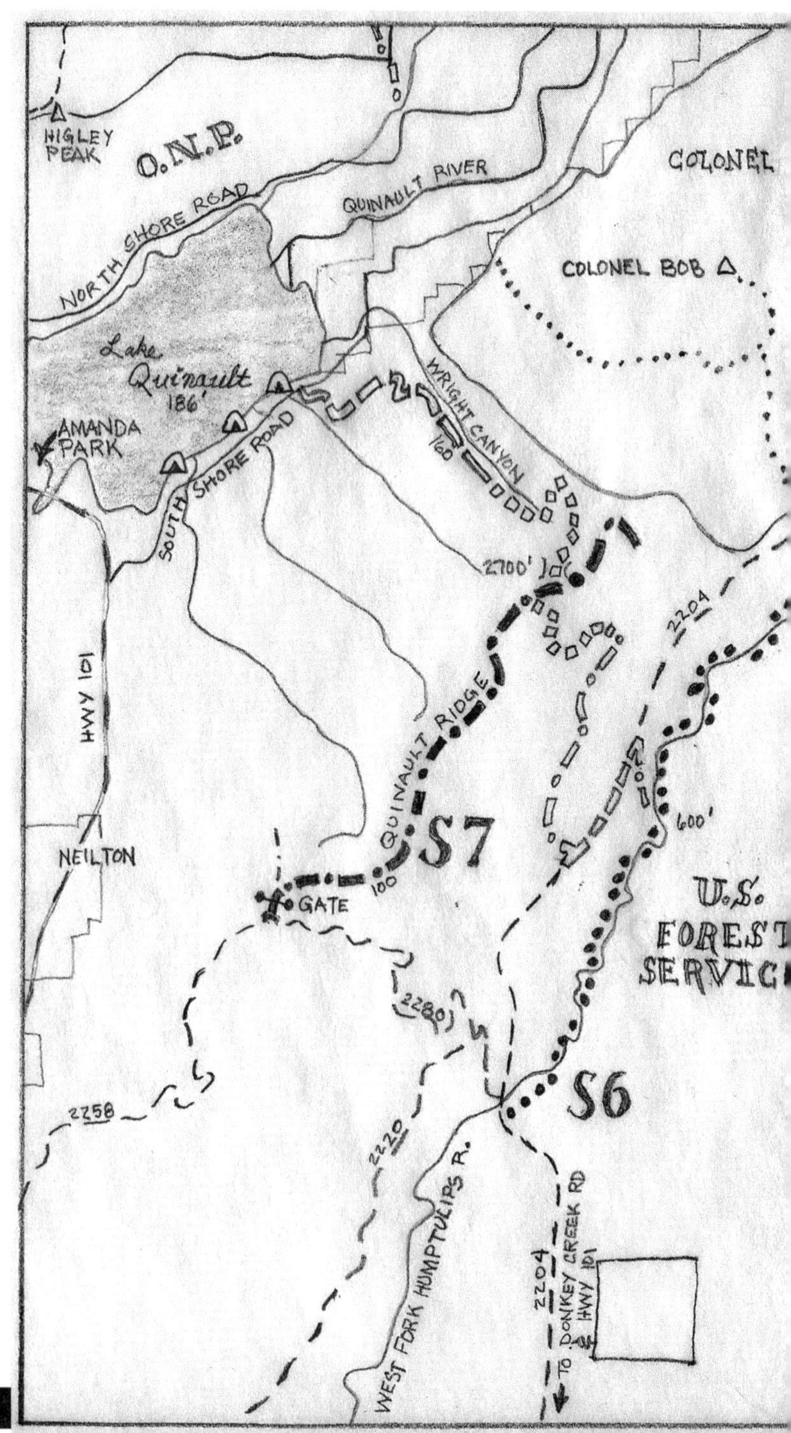

HIGLEY PEAK
O.N.P.
NORTH SHORE ROAD
QUINAULT RIVER
COLONEL
COLONEL BOB
Lake Quinault
186'
AMANDA PARK
SOUTH SHORE ROAD
WRIGHT CANYON
160
2700'
2204
HWY 101
QUINAULT RIDGE
600'
NEILTON
S7
100
GATE
U.S. FOREST SERVIC
2280
2258
2220
S6
WEST FORK HUMPTULIPS R.
2204
TO DONKEY CREEK RD HWY 101

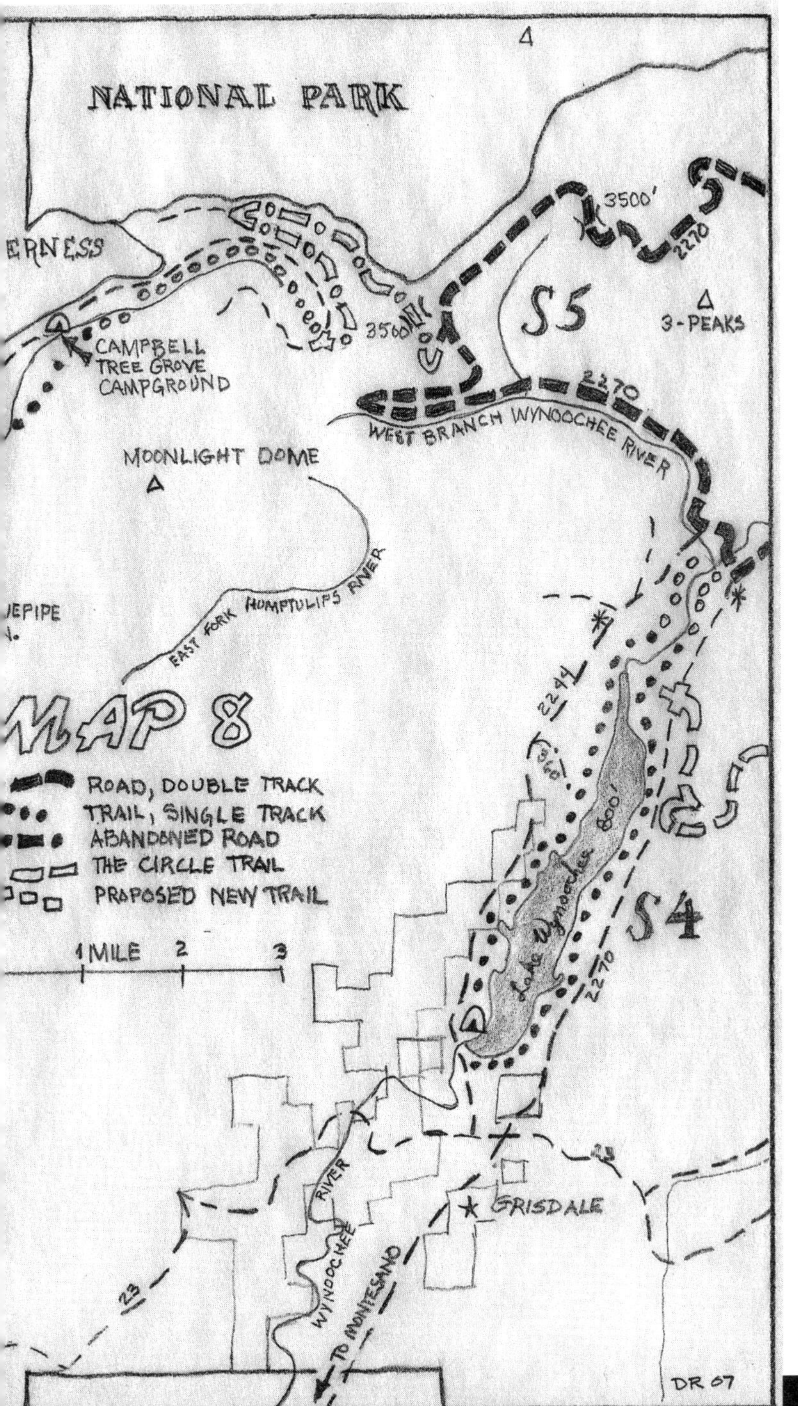
NATIONAL PARK
ERNESS
3500'
2270
S5
3-PEAKS
3500
CAMPBELL
TREE GROVE
CAMPGROUND
2270
WEST BRANCH WYNOOCHEE RIVER
MOONLIGHT DOME
EAST FORK HUMPTULIPS RIVER
JEPIPE
MAP 8
ROAD, DOUBLE TRACK
TRAIL, SINGLE TRACK
ABANDONED ROAD
THE CIRCLE TRAIL
PROPOSED NEW TRAIL
1 MILE 2 3
2270
S4
Lake Wynoochee
800'
23
GRISDALE
WYNOOCHEE RIVER
TO MONTESANO
23
DR 07

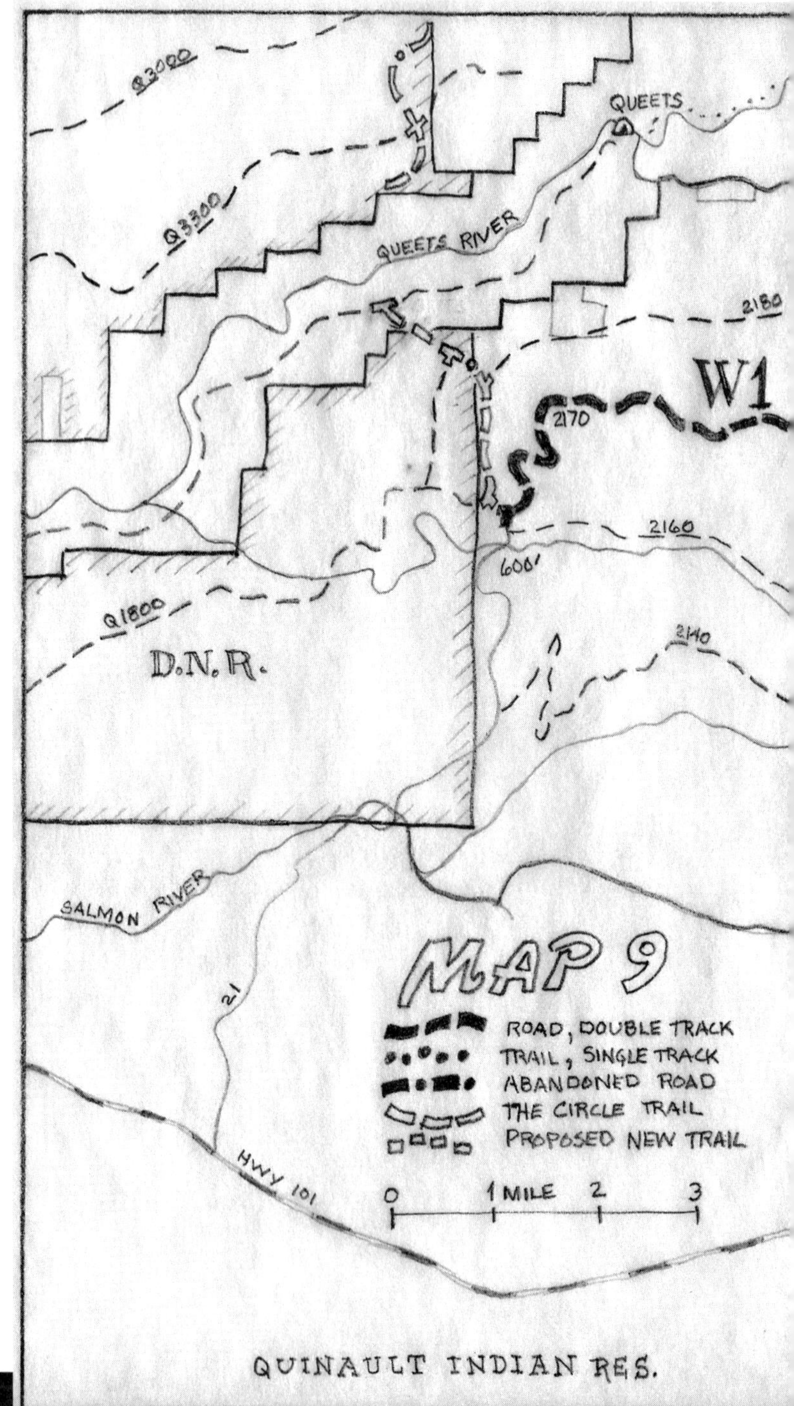

Q3000
Q3300
QUEETS
QUEETS RIVER
2180
W1
2170
2160
600'
2140
Q1800
D.N.R.
SALMON RIVER
21
MAP 9
ROAD, DOUBLE TRACK
TRAIL, SINGLE TRACK
ABANDONED ROAD
THE CIRCLE TRAIL
PROPOSED NEW TRAIL
HWY 101
0
1 MILE
2
3
QUINAULT INDIAN RES.

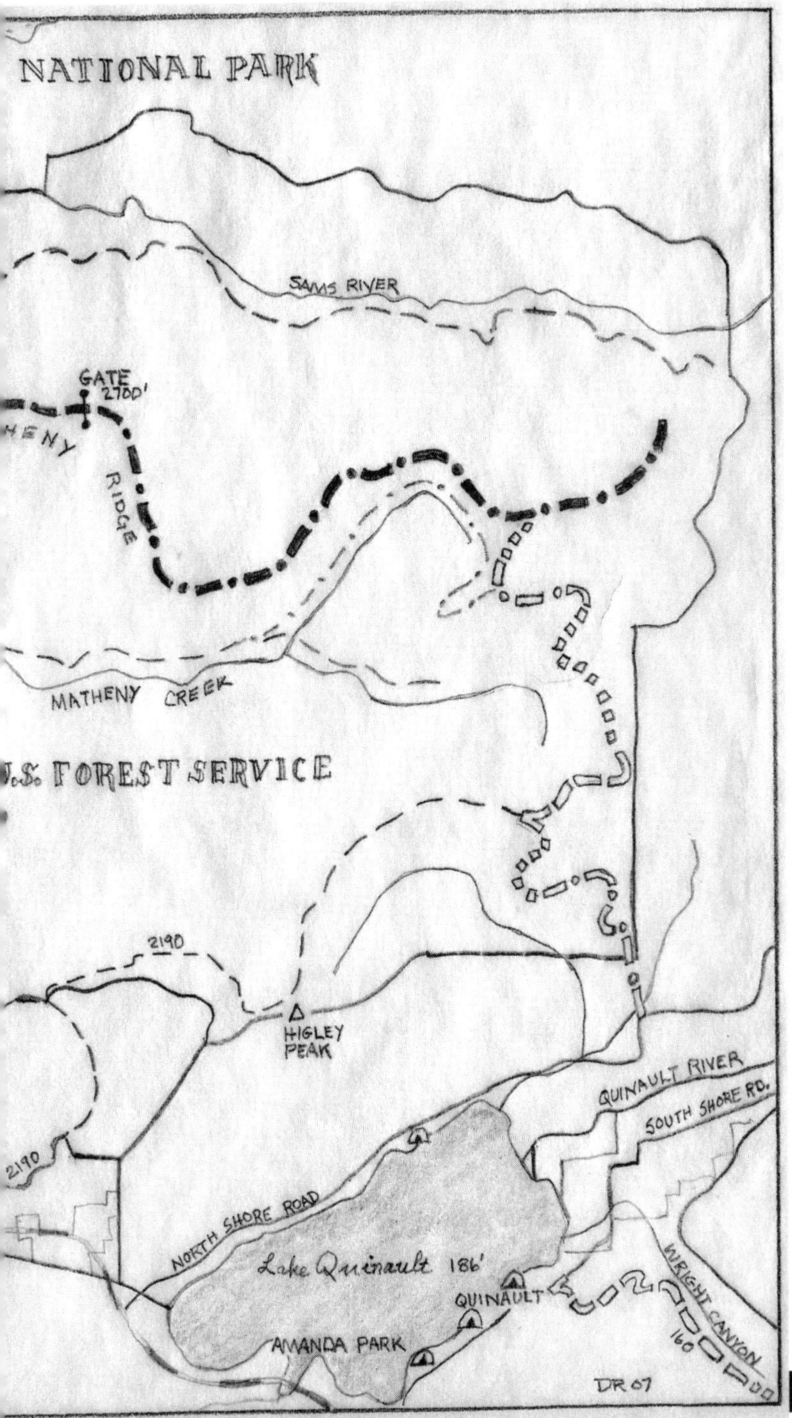
NATIONAL PARK
SAMS RIVER
GATE
2700'
HENY
RIDGE
MATHENY CREEK
U.S. FOREST SERVICE
2190
HIGLEY PEAK
2190
QUINAULT RIVER
SOUTH SHORE RD.
NORTH SHORE ROAD
Lake Quinault 186'
QUINAULT
WRIGHT CANYON
160
AMANDA PARK
DR 07

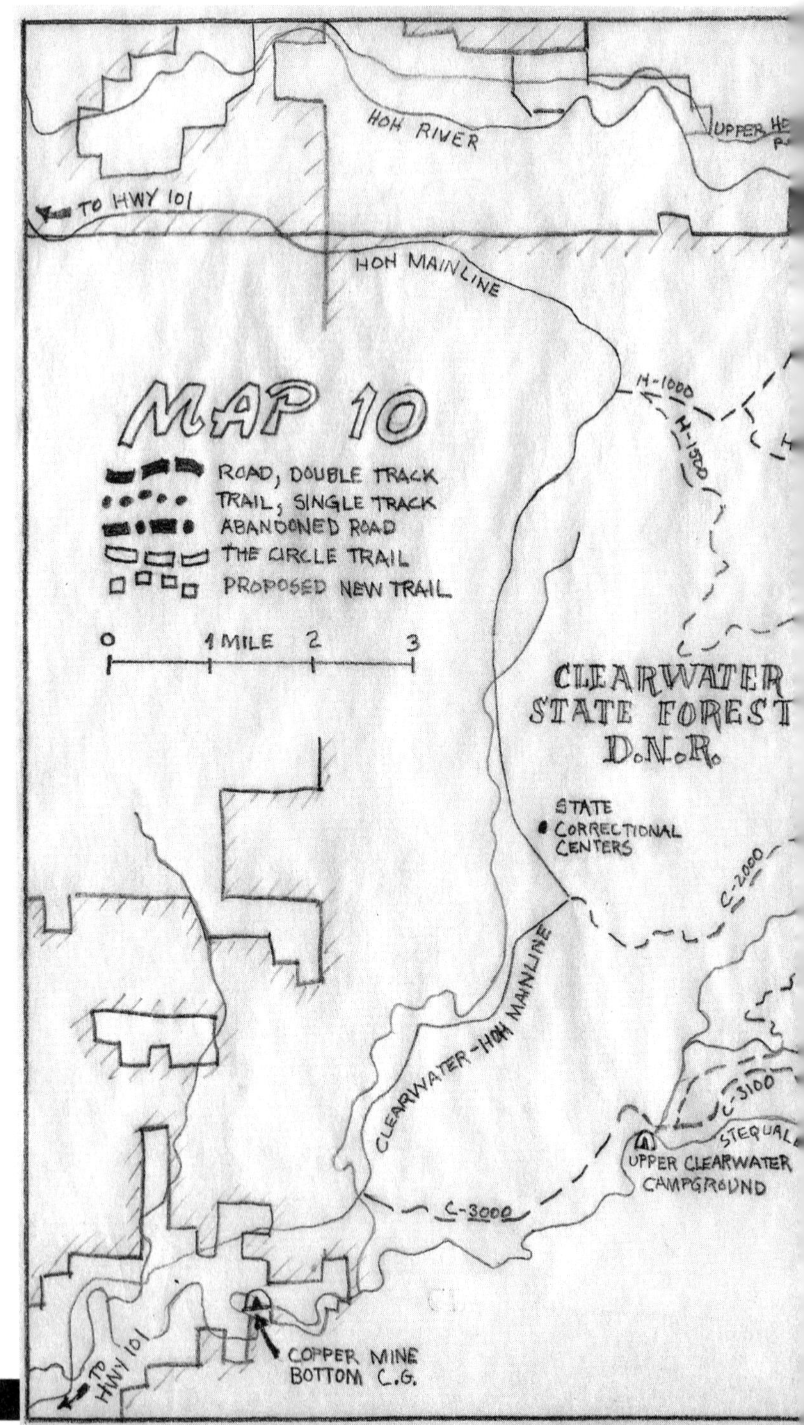
HOH RIVER
UPPER HO
TO HWY 101
HOH MAINLINE
H-1000
H-1500
MAP 10
ROAD, DOUBLE TRACK
TRAIL, SINGLE TRACK
ABANDONED ROAD
THE CIRCLE TRAIL
PROPOSED NEW TRAIL
0
1 MILE
2
3
CLEARWATER
STATE FOREST
D.N.R.
STATE
CORRECTIONAL
CENTERS
C-2000
CLEARWATER-HOH MAINLINE
C-3100
STEQUAL
UPPER CLEARWATER
CAMPGROUND
C-3000
COPPER MINE
BOTTOM C.G.
TO
HWY 101

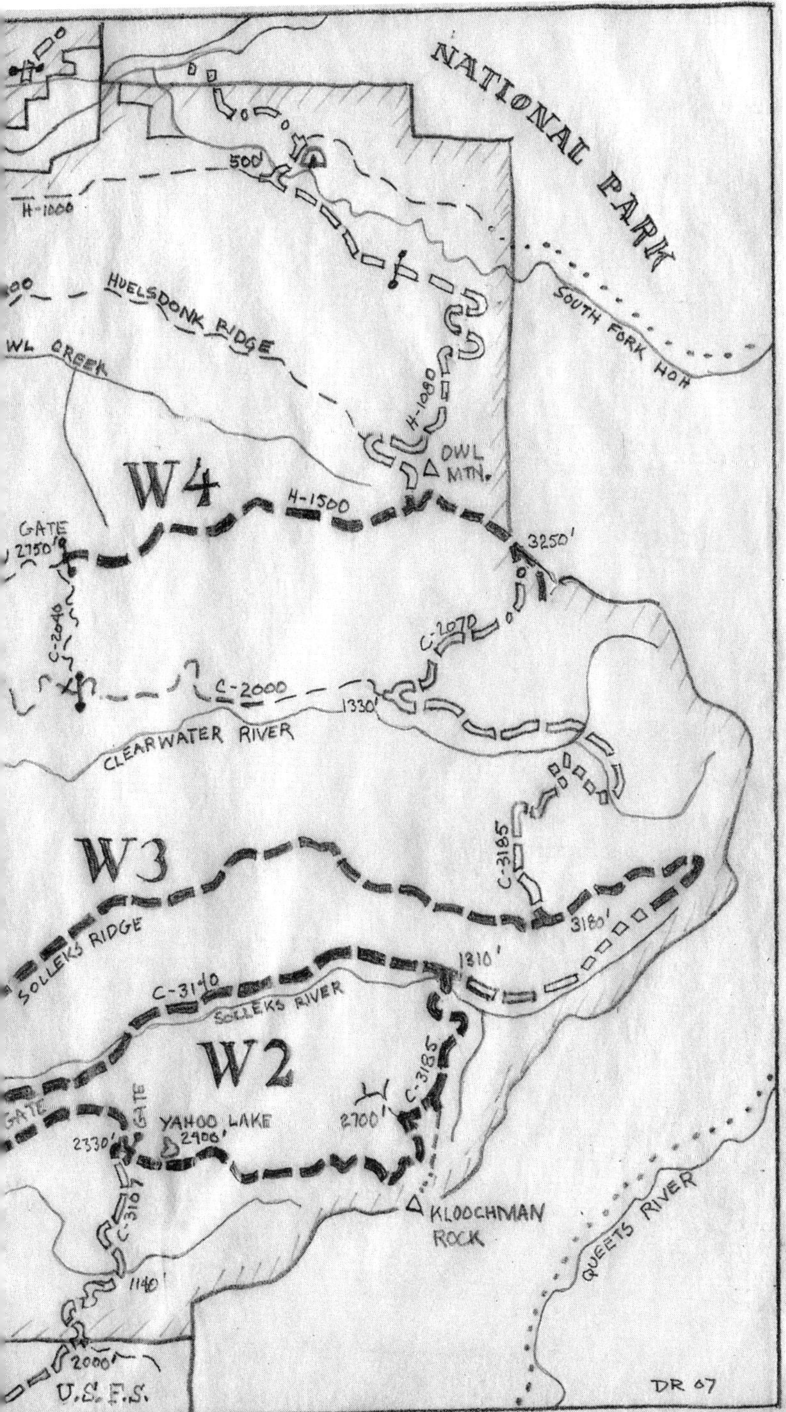
NATIONAL PARK
500'
H-1000
HUELSDONK RIDGE
OWL CREEK
SOUTH FORK HOH
H-1080
OWL MTN.
W4
H-1500
GATE
2750'
3250'
C-2040
C-2070
C-2000
1330'
CLEARWATER RIVER
C-3185
W3
3180'
SOLLEKS RIDGE
1310'
C-3140
SOLLEKS RIVER
W2
C-3185
GATE
GATE
YAHOO LAKE
2900'
2700'
2330'
C-3107
KLOOCHMAN ROCK
QUEETS RIVER
1140'
2000'
U.S.F.S.
DR 07

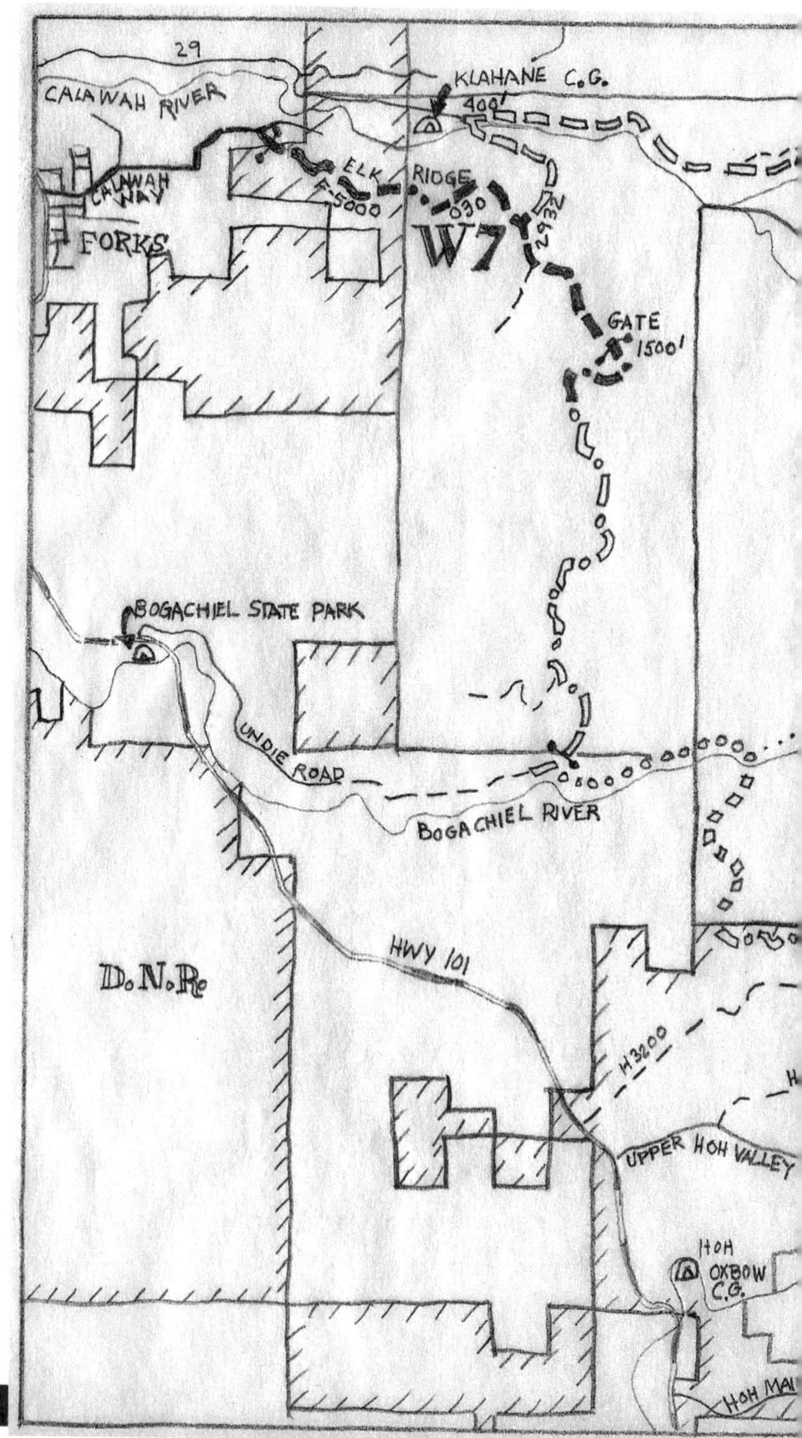
29
CALAWAH RIVER
KLAHANE C.G.
400'
CALAWAH WAY
ELK RIDGE
F-5000
030
FORKS
W7
2932
GATE
1500'
BOGACHIEL STATE PARK
UNDIE ROAD
BOGACHIEL RIVER
HWY 101
D.N.R.
H3200
UPPER HOH VALLEY
HOH OXBOW C.G.
HOH MAI

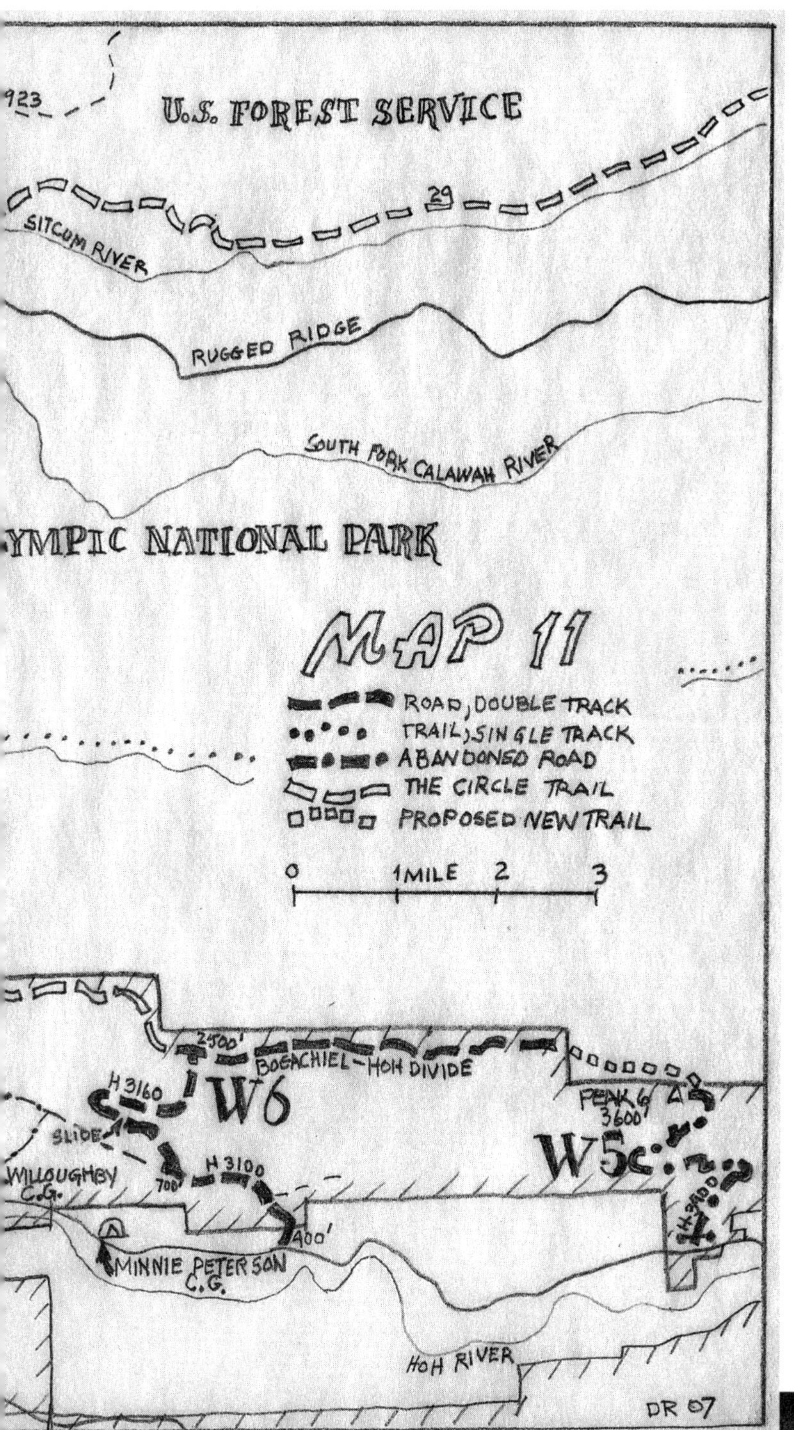
923
U.S. FOREST SERVICE
29
SITCUM RIVER
RUGGED RIDGE
SOUTH FORK CALAWAH RIVER
YMPIC NATIONAL PARK
MAP 11
ROAD, DOUBLE TRACK
TRAIL, SINGLE TRACK
ABANDONED ROAD
THE CIRCLE TRAIL
PROPOSED NEW TRAIL
0
1 MILE
2
3
2500'
BOGACHIEL-HOH DIVIDE
H 3160
W6
SLIDE
WILLOUGHBY C.G.
700'
H 3100
400'
MINNIE PETERSON C.G.
PEAK 6 3600'
W5c
HOH RIVER
DR 07

INDEX